GOD, AS NATURE SEES GOD

GOD, AS NATURE SEES GOD

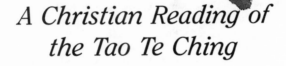

*A Christian Reading of
the Tao Te Ching*

John R. Mabry

•

Illustrations by

Jim Hardesty

ELEMENT

Rockport, Massachusetts • Shaftesbury, Dorset
Brisbane, Queensland

Published in the USA in 1994 by
Element Inc.
42 Broadway, Rockport, MA 01966

Published in Great Britain in 1994 by
Element Books Ltd.
Longmead, Shaftesbury

Published in Australia in 1994 by
Element Books Ltd for
Jacaranda Wiley Ltd.
33 Park Road, Milton, Brisbane, 4064

Text design/composition by Paperwork, Ithaca, New York
Cover design by Max Fairbrother
Printed in the United States by Edwards Brothers, Inc.

Library of Congress Cataloging in Publication data available.
British Library Cataloguing in Publication data available.

ISBN 1-85230-594-0

10 9 8 7 6 5 4 3 2 1

Author and publisher gratefully acknowledge Bear & Co Inc., 506 Agua Fria St.,
Santa Fe, NM, for permission to reprint from: *Meditations with Teilhard de
Chardin*, Blanche Marie Gallagher, ed., © 1988; *Meditations with Nicolas of
Cusa*, James I. Yockey, ed., © 1987; *Meditations with Mechtild of Magdeburg*,
Sue Woodruff, ed., © 1982; *Meditations with Meister Eckhart*, Matthew Fox,
O.P., ed., © 1983; *Meditations with Julian of Norwich*, Brendan Doyle, ed., ©
1983; and *Meditations with Hildegard of Bingen*, Gabriel Uhlein, OSF, ed., ©
1983.
Permissions have been applied for on: *Meditations with John of the Cross*,
Camille Anne Campbell, ed., © 1979; *Meditations with Dante Alighieri*, James
Collins, ed., © 1984; *Behold the Spirit*, Alan Watts, Random House, New York,
© 1972; and *The Tao Te Ching: A New English Version*, Stephen Mitchell,
Harper and Row, New York, © 1988.

CONTENTS

Acknowledgments 7

Foreword by Matthew Fox 9

Introduction 13

The *Tao Te Ching* 23

   1. The Nature of the Tao 107

   2. Paradox 115

   3. Desire 123

   4. Non-action 130

   5. Leadership 138

   6. Oneness 147

   7. World and Self 159

   8. Holiness 170

Epilogue 181

Notes 185

To Shawn Lynn
and his "dog-eared" copy

ACKNOWLEDGMENTS

T HIS BOOK could not have been written without the friendship and guidance of several wise and wonderful people who mentored me through my twenties: Earl Westfall, who nurtured me through my "coming out" of fundamentalism; Ralph Handen, who bought me my first copy of *Original Blessing*; Margaret Dana, who introduced me to Charles Williams; and Catherine Browning McNeely for believing in me. Most especially I wish to thank Cherrisa Mabry for her patience, love, and support.

FOREWORD

by Matthew Fox

THE late Bede Griffith was a deep ecumenist in practice as well as theory. He lived simply as a Christian monk in southern India for fifty years. The ashram he founded there honored Hindu ways while being a Christian monastery at the same time. He was deeply enamoured of the *Tao Te Ching*, calling it perhaps the finest book in the world. Holding his hand up, he would give his own metaphor for deep ecumenism: "If you look at religions as they present themselves to us, it is like five separate fingers. But if you penetrate to their source—to the palm of the hand—you will find they all spring from the same source and instead of being separate entities they are, at their base, sharing in one common, mystical tradition."

I fully concur with Father Griffith's assessment: When religion operates at a superficial level, all is separate; Babel happens; communication suffers. But at their depths religions *ought* to be teaching us spirituality and mysticism and, when they do, they are not in competition with each other. Indeed, a common language emerges when all draw from the same and single source of what Meister Eckhart called "the underground river" and what we might call the "living waters of wisdom." All this I call "deep ecumenism," the coming together of the wisdom traditions of the earth, a coming together especially needed at this critical moment in history.

The *Tao Te Ching* is indeed a beautiful and wise source for a living mysticism, a vital spirituality in our time as East meets West, North meets South, and as crises of despair, alienation, and ecological devastation confront all peoples and all nations. It is a time for wisdom to emerge anew, and it is fitting that a text as profound as the *Tao Te Ching* finds many translations and many interpretations from Westerners to make it more accessible to a greater and greater number of persons. John Mabry brings special perspectives to his translation and interpretation, especially a sensitivity to Christians who up to now have not been exposed to much of the Eastern spiritual wisdom. He is a fellow "journeyer" who is excited about the possibilities that lie ahead. His own religious quest has taken him from the fundamentalism of the Southern Baptists, by way of the Episcopal Church, to ordination as an independent Catholic priest. Rev. Mabry's extensive studies in the religions of the East and his spiritual and religious grounding in the Christian tradition, make him a deep ecumenist of considerable erudition. For the past four years he has been managing editor of *Creation Spirituality* magazine, where he writes a column on the world's religions with an emphasis on the religious and philosophical traditions of the East. In this book, he writes for us in an easy and inviting manner which makes this encounter between the *Tao* and Christianity memorable. He makes a very needed and important contribution.

I myself find the finest way to translate the *Tao* into Western spiritual language is to compare it to what the great mystics such as Meister Eckhart and Thomas Aquinas called the "Godhead." (Borrowing as they did from the fifth century Syrian monk, Denis the Areopagite.) The "Godhead" is the other face of Divinity—other, that is, than "God." God acts but the Godhead does not act; God is God of history but the Godhead is the mystery; God becomes but the Godhead just is; God is "masculine" in both Latin and German; but Godhead is feminine in both languages. God is Creator and Liberator/Redeemer but the Godhead is the Source, indeed the "Source without a Source."

All beings come from the Godhead and return to it at death. In the Godhead there is perfect unity. A recovery of this dimension of Divinity in Western theology and theology schools would do much to advance rapprochement with the East and to awaken our own mystical lives. John Mabry's translation and commentary on the *Tao Te Ching* contributes heartily to this revival of our own mystical heritage at its best. I welcome his significant contribution.

MATTHEW FOX
Holy Names College
Oakland, California
June, 1994

INTRODUCTION

AT a used book store several years ago, on a whim I purchased a copy of Raymond M. Smullyan's book *The Tao is Silent*. I had heard of the Tao, and was intrigued by the little information I had. I had not heard of the *Tao Te Ching*, but I soon gained respect for Taoism's philosophy as Smullyan interpreted it. Halfway through the book a friend came for a visit and saw it. His jaw dropped open and he looked at me in an odd way. "Are you . . . into the Tao?" he said tentatively. "Well," I replied, "I like what I've read."

"Have you read the *Tao Te Ching*?"

"No, but I wa . . ." Before I could finish he dashed out of the house and slammed the door. I contemplated this peculiar behavior and wondered if perhaps I had overlooked a manic tendency in my friend. I certainly hoped he wouldn't hurt himself. Before I could finish my musings, the door had swung wide open once again. My friend hovered in the frame with a crazed look, clutching an enormous dog-eared trade paperback.

"This," he said, panting, pressing the book to my chest, "is the holy word of God."

"You don't say," I returned, flipping through the treasured tome.

It was Gia-Fu Feng and Jane English's translation, beautifully illustrated with Chinese calligraphy and Ms. English's stunning nature photography. "Can I borrow it?" I asked.

He chewed his lip a moment and I had my first glimpse of how terribly important this book really was to him. "I would really love to read through it. It's not long. I'll get it back to you soon. Promise." I lied. From the first few chapters I was entranced with the book's simplicity and awesome profundity. Living with it has seriously affected my life, both spiritually and socially. And this is not an uncommon phenomenon, either. Again and again I have watched people who were profoundly touched evolve toward spiritual maturity.

What is the Tao Te Ching?

The *Tao Te Ching* is a book of Chinese philosophical poetry, written sometime between the seventh and the fourth centuries B.C.E. According to tradition it was written by a quiet librarian named Lao Tzu, which in Chinese can mean, curiously enough, either Old Man or Old Child. Lao Tzu was said to be a contemporary of Confucius, although many years his senior, and the legend of their ideological rivalry is very popular. It is said that both their reputations traveled before them, so when they met face-to-face Lao Tzu was anything but impressed. He sternly rebuked Confucius for his arrogance, greed, and ambition. When the audience was over, Confucius is recorded as saying:

> I understand how birds can fly, how fishes can swim, and how four-footed beasts can run. Those that run can be snared, those that swim may be caught with hook and line, those that fly may be shot with arrows. But when it comes to the dragon, I am unable to conceive how he can soar into the sky riding upon the wind and clouds. Today I have seen Lao Tzu and can only liken him to a dragon.[1]

As the legend goes, Lao Tzu, in his old age, finally gave up on humanity as a lost cause. He packed his yak, and headed for the wilderness where things were sane. At the top of a mountain pass, the last outpost of civilization, the gatekeeper persuaded Lao Tzu to commit his philosophy to paper before he left humankind forever. The resulting book, consisting of just over five thousand Chinese characters, became the famous *Tao Te Ching*, which means "the book of the Way and its power."

Scholars nowadays doubt the historicity of the person Lao Tzu and many believe the book to be a composite work collected by an early Taoist school. This is not universally accepted, though, and once one begins to explore this issue one finds oneself buried up to the neck with the same source and textual criticisms that surround Moses and the Pentateuch. In the end, it is equally irrelevant. Whether Moses wrote the first five books of the Bible or not, does not change the fact that we have this text in our hands and we must, to the best of our abilities and according to the measure of our faith, deal with it. Ultimately, considerations of authorship seem negligible compared to the impact of these words on my lived experience.

What is Taoism?

This is the simplest of questions, and as a typical example of Taoist paradox, almost impossible to answer—mostly because there are many answers. When Thomas Merton was asked, he replied that the only correct answer is "I don't know."[2] Alan Watts, in his excellent book *Tao: The Watercourse Way,* offers a simple and sufficient definition: Taoism is "the way of man's cooperation with the course or trend of the natural world." That's it. There is nothing inherently spiritual about it. There is nothing in Taoism that relies on some form of divine revelation, nothing that any sensitive human being could not learn by simply observing nature. And that is part of its magic: its simplicity. Lao Tzu was not a man to be impressed by political status or educational degrees. To him, maids or stable boys who were true to their own instincts were the noblest sorts of creatures.

Taoism is not a fixed or solid tradition. There are many versions of Taoism. For instance, there is popular Taoism as practiced today which is a highly developed shamanistic religion like many native religions. There is also what Huston Smith calls Esoteric Taoism, which merged with Buddhism over a thousand years ago and evolved into the Ch'an school of Buddhism, known in Japan as Zen. Esoteric Taoism no longer exists as a living, practiced religion separate from Zen or Ch'an. What we are left with, then, is Philosophical Taoism, which is as close as we are likely to get to "original Taoism." It is with this that we are primarily concerned here.

Taoism does not rest on a particular set of scriptures which it considers inspired, but more on a way of looking at the universe suggested by the ancient mystics in their poetry. The most important of these are *Chuang Tzu, Lieh Tzu,* and of course the *Tao Te Ching.* According to legend, Chuang Tzu was a disciple of Lao Tzu, and his works, in a very different style, serve to clarify and augment Lao Tzu's teachings, although at times they seem contradictory. We should not balk at this, though, for often Lao Tzu's own words are blatantly at odds and this is typical of the Taoist spirit: "True words seem paradoxical."

If I seem to be evasive on this, it is not intentional. It is just that Taoism is a terribly slippery subject about which little can be said with universal certainty. Philosophic Taoism holds no dogma, has no organizational structure, no priesthood or clergy, no scripture as such, no creedal formulas or anything else that resembles religious trappings for us.

It is partly for this reason that Taoism is so attractive. It is, in a way, a very non-threatening philosophy to people of other faith traditions because it imposes no doctrine or even metaphysics which could irreconcilably clash with the doctrines that peoples of various faith traditions, Christianity included, might hold.

Why should Christians bother to study Taoism?

Throughout her history, the European Church has ignored and often persecuted other faith traditions that lacked Christianity's political power. When contact was made, the Church's standard response was to convert practitioners by all means necessary and, not infrequently, these means included violence. In medieval Europe, during a period of a hundred years the Holy Inquisition murdered nine million women, worshippers of the Earth as the Great Mother, accusing them of Satanic witchcraft. Upon Cortez's arrival in the western hemisphere the native population of what is now South America was literally massacred, going from 80,000 to 10,000 in a period of just ten years. Fortunately we have, though only in this last century, found less destructive methods of coping with these strangers in our midst. We are no longer isolated from the world at large and the strategies of the past will no longer suffice.

Our present strategies, though less messy, have not yet become very mature. Now this oppression manifests in our words, continuing to perpetuate a tradition of misinformation that invites no real understanding and allows for little compassion. If we are going to live together as a global community, we must discover not only tolerance but respect and understanding. For there is no respect without the will to understand. Ignorance today is consciously and unconsciously erected between adherents of various faith traditions, and these are walls which, if we are going to survive peacefully, must come down.

People are not Hindus because they have been ignorant of the Gospel. A person's choice to become or remain a Hindu can be made intelligently even if Christianity has been honestly explored as a valid faith. And this person's conviction may very well have been made carefully, consciously, and with pure intention. Few Christian leaders are willing to trust their flocks to valid investigation of other faith traditions. If any faith is valid, if it really holds water, what have we to fear? And think of how much we stand to gain as a result of our considerations; a community where the integrity of the person and the tradition is respected and celebrated, where religious prejudice is only a receding memory and the dream of freedom of religion can finally begin to really bloom. We must not deceive ourselves that we have achieved religious freedom. This is only going to come about by compassion and a true willingness to understand and communicate.

Where do we start?

We start by creating open hearts. We start by listening first and talking second. Then we can begin effective dialogue. Fortunately, there has been a great interest in interfaith dialogue in the last fifty years, and we need to begin to see this as vitally important to the living out of our faith and to the future of our planet.

Indian theologian Amarjit Singh Sethi writes that he sees four objectives for interfaith dialogue:

A shared quest for intellectual clarity and understanding.

An encounter on the level of a common humanity.

A shared involvement in the secular community.

A common quest for ultimate reality, or God. [3]

The first objective, an intellectual understanding, can be very revealing and even painful for us, for it will require us to begin to see ourselves from the viewpoint of other faith traditions, and it will most certainly entail a vision of the Church as a very human and often corrupt institution. We will also find, as we share our faiths, that we have much to learn from one another. One thing that the Western traditions (Judaism, Islam, and Christianity) can learn from the East is living peacefully with religious plurality. Hinduism and Buddhism have co-existed for hundreds of years in a spirit of harmony and respect. They also have much to learn from us in the way of historical analysis of faith traditions and their religious evolutions.

Another benefit of dialogue is the discovery of how very much we have in common. Mythologists such as Joseph Campbell have devoted their lives to the comparative study of the mythological heritage of diverse cultures. What results from this is an almost spooky commonality of symbols and images from the most disparate parts of the globe: the creation, the flood, the concept of "the chosen people," the myth of the dying god and his eventual resurrection to life. (It was the dying god myth in fact that convinced C.S. Lewis of Christianity's truth, the other myths being shadows and reflections of the historical Jesus of Nazareth, in whom all of these myths were played out upon the stage of history.)

Let us not also forget the many things the great faith traditions share in common: themes in our scriptures, the existence of monastic communities, the practice of using prayer beads as an aid to memory, and so on. One of the rewards that comes from dialogue happens when you come to understand "the meaning that an alien symbol has had for an alien community, you may discover therein a meaning—of life, of the universe, of man's destiny, or whatever— that was in your own heritage all along but that previously you personally had not seen."[4] This kind of discovery can usher in radical renewal for the person as well as the community of faith.

Isn't it dangerous to go changing things?

It's dangerous not to! A conscious and critical examination of one's faith reveals how very much our traditions have evolved over the centuries. Like anything else in the field of human endeavor, the Christian tradition is not a fixed set of intellectual propositions unbuffeted by the winds of time and political upheaval, but an ever fluid, ever evolving organism clustered around a nucleus of a few ideological convictions that has moved and changed and grown in accordance with the situational needs, and crises, of its people.

A fine example of how a tradition can evolve is found in the Judaic notions of the afterlife. For most of the Old Testament period all souls went to Sheol, the place of the dead, which was not much speculated upon until late in this tradition's development. For the Jews, the afterlife was not important; it was a mystery left in God's hands. What mattered was the Now. How well a person followed God in this life was what was important. Only much later did the Jews develop the concept of Abraham's bosom, and not until the last two centuries before Christ did the ideas of Heaven and resurrection appear in Judaic writings.

Many of the theological concepts we inherited from the Jews are not even Hebraic in origin, but were borrowed and adapted from neighboring religions. For instance, not until the Jews were exiled to Persia do we see a hierarchical structure for angels and demons. These were exclusively Persian concepts until the Jews augmented their own theology with them, and subsequently bequeathed them to us. John S. Dunne shows us that

> In the Bible we have scriptures of different cultural epochs side by side, each characterized by a different philosophy of

life and death and by a different name for God. There is the patriarchal epoch when God was called El and men looked to him for posterity; then there is the subsequent era when he was called Yahweh and men looked to him for the land; and then there is the time when Jesus called him Abba and men looked to him for a kingdom.[5]

It is fairly easy for Christians to see the evolution of Judaism and the transition from it to Christianity, but we have a tough time with that kind of theological fluctuation after the first century. Why is this? Has the evolution of our theology remained stagnant? Hardly! Why have we such trouble conceiving of the Holy Spirit's continued ministry and progressive revelation to the Church in our experiences through time? Have we not encountered God and have we not grown? What have we to fear? The truth is that, although it might be true that God has not changed, human notions of what God is have never ceased changing. Even within the strictest denominations, where everything is concretely defined, you will find as many distinctive theologies as you will members: No two conceptions of God are alike. And everyone's idea of God has a legitimate place in the history of humankind's conception of the Divine.

As scholars such as W.C. Smith have asserted, it is important that we see ourselves not just as part of the history of Christianity, but as part of the total, global history of religion. It is one history, each culture seeking out the divine, each tradition a thread woven together to make a glorious tapestry we call the history of humanity's religion. For religion, in whatever form it is found, is the living and vital relation of humanity to the Divine, no matter how Divinity may be conceived. Teilhard de Chardin has written,

> Religion is not a strictly individual crisis—or choice, or intuition—but represents the long disclosure of God's being through the collective experience of the whole of humanity . . . God bent over the now intelligent mirror of Earth to impress on it the first marks of beauty.[6]

It is imperative that we extend our theological feelers and really explore. For this is one of the most important challenges Christendom faces today, and as our globe grows smaller its urgency will most certainly increase. We need truly creative approaches, and we should not be afraid to explore new areas. Remember that every significant theological advance in Western religious history was initially scorned by the orthodox as heresy. This should not deter us, for we shall be in the company of such heretics as Jesus, Paul, Martin Luther, St. Francis, St. Thomas Aquinas, Martin Luther King, Jr., and the Liberation theologians. And let us remember that the Holy Spirit breathes on us at every moment and has been with us since Pentecost. We should not be afraid, but bold; for our mission is the Gospel of Peace. We should not be afraid to make mistakes, either, for we can trust the Spirit to show us our errors.

> The holy man of our time, it seems, is not a figure like Gotama [Buddha] or Jesus or Mohammed, a man who could found a world religion, but a figure like Gandhi, a man who passes over by sympathetic understanding from his own religion to other religions and comes back again with new insight to his own. Passing over and coming back, it seems, is the spiritual adventure of our time.[7]

I ask the reader now to enter with me into the text of Lao Tzu's *Tao Te Ching*. By reading this before going on to the discussions that follow, you will be able to imbibe much of the *Tao Te Ching*'s deeper meanings. As Thomas Merton has eloquently expressed:

> What wisdom Asia teaches! "Everything is emptiness and everything is compassion." *Asia*. It says everything; it needs nothing. And because it needs nothing it can afford to be silent, unnoticed, undiscovered. It does not need to be discovered. It is we who need to discover it.[8]

TAO TE CHING

道可道
非常道
名可名
非常名

1

The Tao that can be described in words is not the true Tao
The Name that can be named is not the true Name.

From non-existence were called Heaven and Earth
From existence all things were born.

In being without desires, you experience the wonder
But by having desires, you experience the journey.
Yet both spring from the same source and differ mostly
    in name.

        This source is called "Mystery"
        Mystery upon Mystery,
        The womb giving birth to all of being.

2

When people see beauty as beautiful,
They recognize other things as ugly.

When people see goodness as good,
They recognize other things as being bad.

Therefore existence and non-existence produce one another
       Difficult and easy achieve each other
       Long and short define each other
       High and low rely on each other
Voice and accompaniment harmonize with one another
Front and back follow each other.

Therefore, the Sage acts without "doing"
And teaches without words.
       All things arise and she does not refuse them.
       She creates, but does not possess
       Accomplishes, but takes no credit
       When finished, she doesn't dwell on it.
Because she does not dwell on it, it is always present.

3

Do not exalt people who are extraordinarily talented
Or the people will become competitive.

> Do not value precious goods
> Or the people will become thieves.

Do not make a public display of riches and finery
Or the people's hearts will be envious and discontent.

Therefore, the wise leader will empty their hearts of coveting
and fill their bellies with sustenance.
> He discourages their ambition
> and strengthens their bones.
If the people are simple and free from desire,
the crafty will not dare to take advantage of them.

By practicing "not doing," nothing will remain undone.

4

The Tao is like an empty pitcher,
Poured from, but never drained.
Infinitely deep, it is the source of all things.

It blunts the sharp,
Unties the knotted,
Shades the bright,
Unites with all dust.

Dimly seen, yet eternally present,
I do not know who gave birth to it,
It is older than any conception of God.

5

Heaven and Earth are impartial,
They allow things to die.

The Sage is not sentimental,
She knows that all beings must pass away.

The space between Heaven and Earth is like a bellows
Empty, yet inexhaustible
The more it is used, the more it produces.

Trying to explain it will only exhaust you.
It is better to hold on to paradox.

6

The spirit of emptiness is eternal.
It is called "the Mysterious Woman."

Her womb is called "the Source of Heaven and Earth."

Dimly seen, yet eternally present
It is always there for you to use. It's easy!

7

Heaven is eternal, and Earth is long-lasting.
Why are they so enduring?
Because they do not live for themselves.

Therefore the Sage puts himself last
And finds himself in the foremost place.
He does not promote himself, thus he is preserved.

Because he has no thought of "self,"
He is perfectly fulfilled.

8

The sagely person is like water
Water benefits all things and does not compete with them.
It gathers in unpopular places.
In this it is like the Tao.

> In dwelling, live close to the Earth.

> In thinking, be open to new ideas.

> In relationships, be kind.

> In speech, tell the truth and keep your word.

> In leading people, demonstrate integrity.

> In daily matters, be competent.

> In acting, consider the appropriate timing.

If you do not try to prove yourself superior to others,
You will be beyond reproach.

9

Filling your cup until it overflows
is not as good as stopping in time.

Oversharpen your sword
and it will not protect you very long.

You may fill your halls with gold and jewels
but you cannot keep them safe.

Being rich, highly esteemed and proud
will only bring you trouble.

When you have done a good job, rest.
This is the Way of Heaven.

10

Being both body and spirit,
can you embrace unity and not be fragmented?
Being spiritually focused,
can you become soft, like a newborn baby?
Being clear in mind and vision,
can you eliminate your flaws?
Loving all people and leading them well,
can you do this without imposing your will?
When Heaven gives and takes away,
can you be content to just let things come or go?
And even when you understand all things,
can you simply allow yourself to *be*?

To give birth and nourish,
To make and not own,
To act but not expect something in return,
To grow, yet not demand this of others,
This is the virtue of Mystery.

11

Thirty spokes join together at one hub,
But it is the hole in the center that makes it operable.

Clay is molded into a pot,
But it is the emptiness inside that makes it useful.

Doors and windows are cut to make a room,
It is the empty spaces that we use.

Therefore, existence is what we have,
But non-existence is what we use.

12

Too many colors tax people's vision.

Too many sounds deaden people's hearing.

Too many flavors spoil people's taste.

Thrill-seeking leads people to do crazy things.

The pursuit of wealth just gets in people's way.

Therefore, the Sage provides for her needs,
not her desires.

She renounces the latter, and chooses the former.

13

Success is often as unsettling as failure.

The world's troubles are no more important
than the well-being of your own body.

Why do I say, "Success is often as unsettling as failure?"

> Success strikes us deep.
> It shakes us up to get it.
> It shakes us up to lose it.

Thus, success is really little different than failure,
for both are unsettling.

Why do I say, "The World's greatest troubles are no more
important than the well-being of your own body?"

> The reason I think I have troubles
> is because I have material existence.
> If I had no body, what troubles
> could I possibly have?

What we must do is see the whole world as our "Self."
Only then will we be worthy
of being entrusted with the World.

Only One who values the World as his own body
can truly rely on the World in return.

14

Look for it and it cannot be seen—it is beyond sight.

Listen for it and it cannot be heard—it is beyond hearing.

Grasp at it and it cannot be caught—it is beyond substance.

These three cannot be fully comprehended.

They are fundamentally connected and somehow they are one.

> Its highest isn't bright.
> Its lowest isn't dark.
> It is infinite!

Continually emerging, completely beyond description,
It returns again and again to nothingness.

And this is what nothingness looks like:
It is the image of the absence of being.
(It sounds vague and elusive to me!)

Approach it and you will not see its beginning
Follow it and you will not see its end.

If you cling to the Tao of ancient times
the present will be no problem.
To know the ancient origin is to follow the Tao.

15

The Sages of old were scholars who knew well
the way of subtlety, mystery and discernment.

Their wisdom was beyond comprehension.
Because they were beyond comprehension,
I can only describe their appearance:

They were cautious, as if crossing a river in winter.
They were hesitant, as if fearing danger from all sides,

They were polite, as if they were guests.

They were always growing,
like the puddle from a melting cube of ice.

They were genuine, like an uncarved block of wood.

They were as open-minded as a valley.

They were open to infinite possibilities, like a turbulent storm.

Who can wait for the storm to stop,
to find peace in the calm that follows?

The person who is able to wait patiently in this peace
will eventually know what is right.
Those who respect the Tao do not go to extremes.
Not going to extremes, they are inconspicuous and content.

16

If you can empty yourself of everything,
you will have lasting peace.
Things arise, but I contemplate their return.
Things flourish and grow, and then return to their Source.
To return to the Source is to know perfect peace.
I call this a return to Life.

Returning to Life is a Universal Constant.
Knowing this is illuminating.
Someone who doesn't understand this is in error
and may act dangerously.

But knowing this Constant, you can embrace all things.
Embracing all things, you can treat them fairly.
Treating them fairly, you are noble.
Being noble, you are like the cosmos.
If you are like the cosmos, you are like the Tao.

If you are like the Tao, you will have eternal life,
and you needn't be afraid of dying.

17

The best leader is one that the people are barely aware of.
The next best is one who is loved and praised by the people.
Next comes one who is feared.
Worst is one who is despised.

If the leader does not have enough faith in the people,
They will not have faith in him.

The best leader puts great value in words and says little
So that when his work is finished
The people all say, "We did it ourselves!"

18

When the great Tao is abandoned,
Ideas of "humanitarianism" and "righteousness" appear.
When intellectualism arises
It is accompanied by great hypocrisy.

When there is strife within a family
Ideas of "brotherly love" appear.

When a nation is plunged into chaos
Politicians become "patriotic."

19

Forget "holiness," abandon "intelligence"
and people will be a hundred times better off.

Give up "humanitarianism," put away "righteousness"
and people will rediscover brotherly love and kindness.

Forget "great art," throw away "profit"
and there will be no more thieves.

These things are superficial and are simply not enough.
People need something solid to hold on to.
And here it is:

> Be real.
> Embrace simplicity.
> Put others first.
> Desire little.

20

Forget ambitious acquisition of knowledge,
and your sorrows will end.
How much difference is there between "yes" and "no"?
What is the distinction between "good" and "evil"?
Must I value what others value? Nonsense!
Having no end to their desires, they are desolate.

People rush here and there, maybe going to a feast,
or perhaps climbing a tower in the springtime.
I alone am calm and unconcerned.
Like an unselfconscious infant
At peace and having no destination.

Most people have more than they need.
But I alone seem lost and out of place.
I have the mind of a fool—so confused!

Ordinary people are bright.
I alone seem dim.
Ordinary people are discriminating.
I alone am ambivalent.

> As quiet as the ocean.
> As free as the wind.

People rush about on their very important business.
But I alone seem incorrigible and uncouth.
I am different from ordinary people;
I enjoy feeding from the Great Mother's breasts.

21

The only virtue worth having is that of following the Tao,
and the only thing you can say about the Tao,
is that it is elusive and evasive.

It is elusive and evasive, yet it can be observed.
It is evasive and elusive, yet it does manifest itself.
It is dim and dark, yet its essence can be grasped.

Its essence is unquestionably genuine.
You can put your faith in it.

From the beginning of time until the present,
its Name has remained.
In it one can see all of Creation.
How do I know where all of Creation comes from?
I know the Tao!

22

If you don't want to be broken, bend.
If you want to be straight, allow some crookedness.
If you want to be filled, become empty.
If you want to be made new, let yourself be used.
If you want to be rich, desire little.
Wanting more and more is craziness!

Therefore the Sage embraces oneness
and becomes a model for the world.
Not self-centered, she is enlightened.
Not self-righteous, she is a shining example.
Not self-glorifying, she accomplishes glorious things.
Not boastful, she grows large inside.
She alone does not compete,
And so the world can never overcome her.

When the ancients said, "If you don't want to be broken, bend"
Were they just uttering empty words?
Bend sincerely and wholeness will return to you.

23

Nature uses few words.
So, a whirlwind will not last all morning.
A sudden storm will not last all day.
What causes these?
Heaven and Earth.
If Heaven and Earth need not speak for long,
How much less should humankind?

Therefore, one who seeks the Tao is at one with the Tao.
One who seeks goodness is good.
One who seeks loss is lost.

If you are one with the Tao, the Tao eagerly accepts you.
If you are one with goodness,
goodness is happy to receive you.
If you are one with loss, loss welcomes you.

If you do not trust enough, you will not find trust.

24

One who stands on tiptoe does not stand firm.
One who rushes ahead is likely to trip.
One who listens only to himself cannot learn.
One who considers himself righteous, isn't.
One who brags has nothing to brag about.
One who feels sorry for himself does not grow.

Compared to the Tao, these people are table scraps
and wasted effort,
and not well-liked by anyone or anything.

So, if you follow the Tao, you will not live like that.

25

Before Heaven and Earth were born
There was something undescribable.
Perfectly still, having no form,
It stands alone, and does not change.
It acts perpetually, yet never tires.
It could very well be the Mother of the Universe.
I don't know its name, so I just call it the Tao.
If forced to give it a name, I would call it Great.

> Being Great, I call it eternal.
> Being eternal, I call it infinite.
> Being infinite, I call it Reconciliation.

> Therefore, the Tao is Great.
> Heaven is Great.
> The Earth is Great.
> Humankind is also Great.

In the Universe there are these four things which are Great,
And Humankind is one of them.

> Humankind follows the Earth,
> The Earth follows Heaven,
> Heaven follows the Tao,
> And the Tao just acts like itself.

26

Heaviness is the root of lightness.
Stillness is the master of restlessness.

Therefore, the Sage walks all day
and never parts from the baggage wagon.
Although there are many beautiful palaces to behold,
He is beyond such things and is at peace.

Why should the ruler of ten thousand chariots
Act with such frivolity in this world?
To act lightly is to lose one's root.
To be restless is to lose one's self-control.

27

A skillful walker leaves no tracks.
A skillful speaker makes no mistakes.
A skillful accountant needs no counting-devices.
A well-made door needs no lock, yet cannot be opened.
A well-made binding uses no rope, yet will not be undone.

> Therefore, the Sage is always there to help people
> So that no one is forsaken.
> She is always there to see to things
> So that nothing is lost.
> This is called being clothed in light.

What is a good person but a bad person's teacher?
What is a bad person but raw material for a good person?

If you do not respect your Teacher,
Or love your "raw material,"
You are greatly confused, regardless of your intelligence.

I call this an essential, yet subtle mystery.

28

Know the active, the masculine
Yet keep to the passive, the feminine
And you will cradle the World.
If you lovingly hold the World
You will know eternal goodness
And will become again as a little child.

Be aware of the obvious—the light
But keep to the mysterious—the dark
And set an example for the world.
Be an example for the world
And do not stray from your calling
And you will return to the Eternal.

Know honor, yet remain humble
And be empty of the world.
Being empty of the world is good enough
And you will return to the simplicity of the uncarved block.
If the block is carved it is trapped in one form and critiqued.
The Sage prefers simplicity and so is ahead of them all.
He knows better than to divide the whole.

29

Do you want to own the World and improve it?

I don't think you can.

You see, the World is sacred.
It can't be improved upon.
If you try you will ruin it.
If you try to own it,
You will lose it.

Therefore, sometimes you must lead and sometimes
you must follow.
Sometimes you need to blow hard, and sometimes you
can breathe easily.
Sometimes you must be strong and sometimes tender.
Sometimes you win and sometimes you lose.

Knowing this, the Sage avoids extremes,
extravagances and exhaustion.

30

A leader who is advised to rely on the Tao
Does not enforce his will upon the world by military means.
For such things are likely to rebound.

> Wherever armies have camped
> Thistles and briars grow.
> In the wake of war
> Bad years are sure to follow.

A good leader accomplishes only what he has set out to do
And is careful not to overestimate his ability.

He achieves his goal, but does not brag.
He effects his purpose, but does not show off.
He is resolute, but not arrogant.
He does what he must, though he may have little choice.
He gets results, but not by force.

Things that grow strong soon grow weak.
This is not the Way of the Tao.
Not following the Tao leads to an early end.

31

All weapons are bad news
And all creatures should detest them.
So those who follow the Tao do not keep them.

(Wise people prefer the left side as the place of honor,
but the General always stands on the right.)

Weapons are the tools of fear.
They are not appropriate for a Sage
And should only be one's last resort.
Peace is always far superior.

There is no beauty in victory.
To find beauty in it would be to rejoice at killing people.
Anyone who delights in slaughter will never find
satisfaction in this world.

(When celebrating happy occasions,
  the left side is the place of honor,
But on unhappy occasions, the right is preferred.
Then we see those of lower rank standing on the left;
The General is given the right-hand position.)

Military officers should observe their duties gravely,
For when many people are killed
They should be mourned with great sorrow.
Celebrate your victory only with funeral rites.

32

The Tao will always be beyond comprehension.
Although it seems trivial
No one in all the world can control it.

If governments and leaders can abide in it
All beings shall gratefully behave likewise.
We would have a Heaven on Earth
And sweet rains would fall.
The people would not need to be told,
They would just naturally do what is right.

When you organize, you must of necessity
use names and order.
But given that, you must also know where to leave off
naming and structuring.
Knowing when to stop, you can avoid danger.
All the World is to the Tao
As rivers flowing home to the sea.

33

One who knows others is intelligent.
One who knows himself is truly wise.

One who overcomes others has force.
One who overcomes the self has true strength.

One who knows he has enough is truly wealthy.
One who has discipline is sincere.
One who remembers his Source will endure.
He embraces death and so does not perish
but lives forever.

34

The great Tao flows everywhere,
to the left and to the right.
All things rely on it for their life
and it does not refuse them.
When its work is done, it does not demand recognition.
It clothes and nourishes all things
and does not demand allegiance.

Since it makes no demands for itself,
it can seem to be of small regard.
Yet as all things return to it of their own accord,
without being commanded, it can truly be regarded Great.
It is only because it does not claim to be Great
That it is able to achieve such Greatness.

35

Whoever holds firmly to following the Tao
Will draw all the World to herself.
She may go anywhere and not be afraid,
Finding only safety, balance, and peace.

Music and good food lure passers-by
But words about the Tao
Seem bland and flavorless to them.

Look, and it cannot be seen.
Listen, and it cannot be heard.
Use it, and it cannot be exhausted.

36

What you want shrunk
Must first be allowed to expand.

What you want weakened
Must first be strengthened.

What you want destroyed
Must first be allowed to flourish.

That which you want to take
Must first be given.

Seeing this is an understanding of the subtle.

What is soft and weak overcomes what is hard and strong.

Just as a fish should keep to deep waters,
So a country's weapons should be kept out of sight,
so as not to tempt people.

37

The Tao never "acts"
Yet nothing is left undone.

If the governments and leaders would keep it
All things would of their own accord be transformed.

Should desires arise from transformation
I shall influence them through silent simplicity.
Silent simplicity involves being free from desires.

When you are without desire you are content
And all the World is at peace.

38

A truly good person does not try to be good,
Therefore is he able to be good.

Another person tries to be good,
And finds that he cannot.

A good person does not act, nor has any reason to.
Another person is always doing
because he thinks he has to.

A humanitarian acts from the heart.
A politician acts, but he has ulterior motives.
When a legalist acts and gets no response,
He rolls up his sleeves and uses force.

Therefore, when the Tao is lost,
Remember that there is still goodness.
When goodness is lost, there is still kindness.
When kindness is lost, there is still the law.
When the law is lost, there is still politeness.
Politeness is the thin edge of loyalty and trust,
And is the beginning of chaos.

We need those who try to direct society
About as much as the Tao needs a flower
to make it attractive.
They mark the beginnings of stupidity.

The Sage concerns herself with causes,
Not symptoms
And focuses on the Tao, not the silly flower.
Forget the flower, follow the Tao instead.

39

People of ancient times possessed oneness.
The sky attained oneness and so became clear.
Earth attained oneness and so found peace.
The Spirit attains oneness and so is replenished.
The Valleys attained oneness and so became full.
All things attain oneness and they flourish.
The ancient leaders attained oneness
And so became examples for all the world.

All of this is achieved by oneness.

Without oneness, the sky would crack
The Earth explode
The Spirit exhaust
The Valley deplete
Leaders would certainly fall
And all life perish.

Therefore the Great recognizes the Small as its root.
The High takes the Low as its foundation.
Leaders refer to themselves as orphans and widows.
Is this not grounding oneself in humility?

Therefore the highest renown is no renown.
We do not want to glitter like jewels.
We do not want to be hard as stone.

40

Returning is the movement of the Tao.
Yielding is the way of the Tao.
All things in the world are born of existence.
Existence is born of non-existence.

41

When wise people hear about the Tao
They follow it carefully.
When ordinary people hear about the Tao
They can take it or leave it.
When foolish people hear about the Tao
They laugh out loud.
If they didn't laugh out loud, it wouldn't be the Tao!

Therefore it is said:
The path into light seems dark.
The way ahead seems to go backwards.
The path into peace seems rough.
The greatest good seems to us empty.
True purity seems stained.
The best efforts seem inadequate.
Appropriate caution seems like cowardice.
True essence seems violated.
The truly square bears no corners.
Sound vessels take time to build.
Celestial music is seldom paid much heed.
The ultimate image is impossible to capture.

The Tao is hidden and nameless
Yet it is the Tao alone that nourishes
and completes all things.

42

The Tao gives birth to one.
One gives birth to two.
Two gives birth to three,
And three gives birth to all things.

All things carry Yin and embrace Yang
Desiring nothing and finding harmony.

All people hate loneliness and poverty
Though they are the noblest of states.

So in losing, much is gained,
And in gaining, much is lost.

What others have taught, I also teach:

"The violent shall die with violence."

This is my primary teaching.

43

The softest thing in the World
Overcomes the hardest thing in the World.
That which is without substance can enter
even where there is no space.

Therefore I know the value of non-action.

Teaching without words
And benefit without actions
There are few in the World who can grasp it.

44

Fame or self: which is more important?

Your possessions or your person: which is worth more to you?

Gain or loss: which is worse?

Therefore, to be obsessed with "things" is a great waste,
The more you gain, the greater your loss.

> Being content with what you have been given,
> You can avoid disgrace.
> Knowing when to stop,
> You will avoid danger.
> That way you can live a long and happy life.

45

True perfection seems flawed
Yet its usefulness is never exhausted.

True fulfillment seems empty
Yet its usefulness is infinite.

True straightness seems crooked.
Great skill appears easy.
Great eloquence sounds awkward.

Cold overcomes heat.
Tranquility conquers agitation.
Purity and stillness is the universal ideal.

46

When the World keeps to the Tao
Strong horses are best used to manufacture manure.
When the World forgets the Tao
War horses are bred outside the city.

There is no greater curse than discontent.
Nothing breeds trouble like greed.
Only one who is content with what is enough
will be content always.

47

Without going outside,
You can know the whole world.
Without looking out the window,
You can know Heaven's Way.

The further out you seek
The less you understand.

Therefore, the Sage
Knows without needing to travel,
Understands without needing to see,
Accomplishes without "doing."

48

To pursue learning is to grow a little more every day.
To pursue the Tao is to desire a little less every day.
　　　Desire less and less
　　　Until you arrive at "not-doing."
When you practice "not-doing," nothing is left undone.

If you want to have the whole world, have nothing.
If you are always busy doing something,
you cannot enjoy the world.

49

The Sage's heart is not set in stone.
She is as sensitive to the people's feelings as to her own.

She says, "To people who are good, I am good.
And to people who are not good?
I am good to them, too."
This is true goodness.

"People who are trustworthy, I trust.
And people who are not trustworthy, I also trust."
This is real trust.

The Sage who leads harmoniously considers the mind of
her people as well as her own.
They look to her anxiously.
They are like her own children.

50

From birth to death,
Three people out of ten are celebrators of Life.
Three people out of ten are advocates of Death.
The rest simply move numbly from cradle to grave.
Why is this?

Because they are overly protective of this life.

It is said that one who knows how to protect his life can
walk freely without fear of the wild buffalo or tiger.
He may meet an army bravely with neither sword nor shield.
For the buffalo will find no place to sink its horns,
The tiger finds no place to dig his claws,
Weapons find no soft spot to pierce.
Why?

Because there is no place for death in him.

51

The Tao gives birth to all things.
Nature's goodness nurtures them.
  Matter forms them.
  Environment shapes them.
Therefore, all things cannot help but to
respect the Tao and treasure goodness.
Respect for the Tao and the treasuring of goodness are not
demanded of them, they do it naturally.

So, the Tao gives birth;
Nature's goodness nurtures them,
grows them, raises them and enables them to mature,
ripens them, nourishes and shelters them.

  The Tao gives birth, but does not possess;
  Acts, but does not take credit;
  Guides, but does not control.

  This is the mystery of goodness.

52

The World has an origin
Which we may regard as the Mother of the Universe.
Knowing the Mother, we can also come to know
her children.
Knowing the children, return and hold fast to the Mother.
Doing this, you will not meet with danger
your whole life long.

> Close your mouth
> Go easy on the senses
> And life will not be so hard.

> If you spend your life filling your senses
> And rushing around "doing" things
> You will be beyond hope.

To concern yourself with the beautiful and small
is true wisdom.
To foster gentleness is true strength.
Choose to do what is wise and return to wisdom.
Then you will avoid life's troubles.
This is called practicing consistency.

53

If I possess even a little wisdom
Then while I walk in the light of the Tao
My only fear is that I'll fall into "doing."
The path of the Tao is obvious and simple,
But most people prefer to take short-cuts.

The courts of law are far from the people's hearts.
The fields are full of weeds,
And the storehouses are empty.

But look, here are officials in elegant apparel
carrying sharp swords
Eating and drinking until they are bloated,
Possessed of such wealth that they could never use it all.

I call this positively criminal.
It is not the way of the Tao.

54

One who is well grounded will not be uprooted.
One who has a firm embrace will not let go.
His descendants will faithfully carry on his tradition.

> Cultivate these things in yourself
> And you will have true goodness.
> Cultivate these in your family
> And goodness will increase.
> Cultivate these in your community
> And goodness will catch on.
> Cultivate these in your nation
> And goodness will overflow!
> Cultivate these in the World
> And goodness will fill the Universe.

And so, let the self examine the self.
Let the family consider the family.
Let the community examine the community.
Let the nation evaluate the nation.
Let the World contemplate the World.

> How do I know the World is like this?
> Through these:
>
> Grounding and embracing.

55

One who is filled with goodness is like
a freshly-born infant.
Wasps, scorpions, and snakes will not bite her.
Wild beasts will not attack her,
nor will birds of prey pounce on her.
Her bones may be fragile and her skin soft,
But her grasp is firm.
She does not recognize the union of male and female
For she knows it only as an undivided whole.
This is the essence of perfection.
She can howl all day and not get hoarse.
This is perfect harmony.

> Knowing harmony is faithfulness.
> Knowing faithfulness is salvation.

Trying to extend one's life-span is dangerous and unnatural.
To manipulate one's energy with the mind is a powerful thing
But whoever possesses such strength invariably grows old
and withers.

> This is not the way of the Tao.
> All those who do not follow the Tao will come
> to an early end.

56

Those who know, do not speak.
Those who speak, do not know.

So shut your mouth
Guard your senses
Blunt your sharpness
Untangle your affairs
Soften your glare
Be one with all dust.
This is the mystery of union.

You cannot approach it
Yet you cannot escape it.
You cannot benefit it
Yet you cannot harm it.
You cannot bestow any honor on it
Yet you cannot rob it of its dignity.
That is why the whole Universe reveres it.

57

As a leader, lead properly.
Don't resort to force in the usual ways.
Win the World by "not-doing."
How do I know to do this?

Listen, the more laws and prohibitions there are
The poorer the people become.
The more dreadful weapons you have
The more chaotic the state of the nation.
The more clever and advanced your knowledge
The stranger things become.
The more commandments and regulations you have
The more thieves there are.

Therefore the Sage who leads says:
"I practice 'not-doing' and the people transform themselves.
I enjoy peace and the people correct themselves.
I stay out of their business affairs and the people prosper.
I have no desires and the people, all by themselves,
become simple and honest."

58

When a government is unobtrusive
The people are simple and honest.
When a government is suspicious and strict
The people are discontented and sneaky.

Blessings are rooted in misery.
Misery lurks behind blessing.
Where does it ever end?

There is no such thing as "normal."
What seems normal is only an illusion,
And what seems good is finally revealed to be monstrous.
The people's confusion has lasted a very long time.

Therefore the Sage is honest, but not judgmental
Strong, but not injurious to others
Straightforward, but not reckless
Bright, but not blinding.

59

In leading people and serving Heaven
There is nothing better than moderation.
In moderation, one is already following the Tao.
When one follows the Tao, great goodness is abundant.
When great goodness is in abundance,
There is nothing that cannot be overcome.
When there is nothing that cannot be overcome
Then there are no limits.
Having no limits, one can certainly govern a country.
If you know the country's Mother, you will long endure.

I call this having deep roots and a firm stalk.
This is the Way of long life and great insight.

60

Govern a big country as you would fry a small fish.

Approach the world with the Tao and evil will have no power.
Not that evil has no power, but it will not harm people.

Not that evil is not harmful,
but the Sage is dedicated to not harming people—even evil people.
When no one hurts another,
all will eventually return to the good.

61

A great country is like a low-lying lake where many rivers converge;
A focal point for the Earth, the feminine Spirit of the World.
The female always overcomes the male by stillness.
Stillness is the lowest position.

> Therefore a big country,
> By placing itself below a smaller country
> Will win the smaller country.

> And a small country,
> By placing itself below a larger country
> Will gain the large country.

> Therefore, by being humble, one gains
> And the other, being humble already, also gains.

> A great country needs to embrace the lowly.
> The small country needs to serve others.
> Thus, both needs are satisfied
> And each gets what it wants.

Remember, the great country should always humble itself.

62

The Tao is the bosom of the Universe
It is the good person's treasure
And the bad person's refuge.

Flattery may buy one's position
And good deeds can win people over
But if one's heart is not pure
That is all the more reason to cling to the Tao!

Therefore when a king is coronated,
Crowned in ceremony,
Presented with gifts of rare value,
And escorted in luxury,
All these things pale when compared to the humble gift
of the Tao, offered in silence.

Why did the Sages of old value the Tao so much?
Because when you seek, you find
And when you sin, you are forgiven.

That is why the Tao is the greatest treasure of the Universe.

63

Do without "doing."
Work without forcing.
Taste without seasonings.
Recognize the Great in the small,
And the many in the few.

Repay hatred with kindness.

Deal with the difficult while it is still easy.
Begin great works while they are small.
Certainly the Earth does difficult work with ease,
And accomplishes great affairs from small beginnings.
So, the Sage, by not striving for greatness,
Achieves greatness.

A person who makes promises lightly
Is not regarded as trustworthy.

If you think everything is easy,
You will find only difficulty.
That is why the Sage considers all things difficult
And finds nothing too difficult in the end.

64

What is at rest is easy to maintain.
What has not yet happened is easy to plan.
That which is fragile is easily shattered
That which is tiny is easily scattered.

Correct problems before they occur.
Intervene before chaos erupts.

A tree too big around to hug is produced from a tiny sprout.
A nine-story tower begins with a mound of dirt.
A thousand-mile journey begins with your own two feet.

Whoever tries will fail.
Whoever clutches, loses.

Therefore the Sage, not trying, cannot fail
Not clutching, she cannot lose.

When people try,
they usually fail just on the brink of success.
If one is as cautious at the outset as at the end,
One cannot fail.

Therefore the Sage desires nothing so much
as to be desireless.
She does not value rare and expensive goods.
She unlearns what she was once taught
And helps the people regain what they have lost;
To help every being assume its natural way of being,
And not dare to force anything.

65

In ancient times those who followed the Tao
Did not try to educate the people.
They chose to let them be.

The reason people become hard to govern
Is that they think they know it all.
So, if a leader tries to lead through cleverness,
He is nothing but a liability.
But if a leader leads, not through cleverness,
but through goodness, this is a blessing to all.

To be always conscious of the Great Pattern
is a spiritual virtue.

Spiritual virtue is awesome and infinite
And it leads all things back to their Source.
Then there emerges the Great Harmony.

66

Rivers and the sea are able to rule the streams
of a hundred valleys.
Because they are good at taking the lower position,
The streams of a hundred valleys run to them.

Therefore, if you want to rule effectively over people
You must surely speak as if below them.
If you want to lead well,
You must surely walk behind them.

That way when the Sage takes a position of power
The people will not feel oppressed.
And when the Sage leads
The people will not think he is in the way.

Therefore the whole world joyfully praises him
and does not tire of him.

Because he refuses to compete,
The world cannot compete with him.

67

Everyone says this Tao of mine is great and nebulous.
So great, in fact, that it is too nebulous to be of any use.

I have three treasures that I hold and cherish:
One is called "compassion"
Another is called "moderation"
And the third is called "daring not to compete."

With compassion, one is able to be brave.
With moderation, one has enough to be generous with others.
Without competition, one is fit to lead.

Nowadays people don't bother with compassion
But just try to be brave.
They scoff at moderation
And find they have little enough for themselves.
They step on people in their rush to be first—
This is death!

One who is compassionate in warfare is victorious
And in defense he holds fast.
When Heaven moves to save someone
It protects him through compassion.

68

The best soldier is not violent.
The best fighter is not driven by anger.
The true conqueror wins without confrontation.
The best employer is humble before his employees.

I say there is much good in not competing.
I call it using the power of the people.
This is known as being in tune with Heaven,
Like the Sages of old.

69

The military has a saying:

> "I would rather be passive, like a guest
> than aggressive, like a host.
> I would rather retreat a foot
> than advance an inch."

> This is called going forward without instigating,
> Engaging without force
> Defense without hatred
> Victory without weapons.

There is no greater calamity than underestimating the enemy.
If I take my enemy too lightly, I am in danger of losing my
compassion, moderation, and non-competitive spirit.

So, when two armies confront each other
Victory will go to them that grieve.

70

My words are very easy to understand
And very easy to practice.
Yet the World is not able to understand
Nor able to put them into practice.

My words speak of the primal.
My deeds are but service.
Unless people understand this
They won't understand me.
And since so few understand me,
Then such understanding is rare and valuable indeed.

Therefore the Sage wears common clothes
And hides his treasures only in his heart.

71

She who knows that she does not know is the best off.
He who pretends to know but doesn't is ill.

Only someone who realizes he is ill can become whole.
The Sage is not ill because she recognizes
this illness as illness,
Therefore she is not ill.

72

When people lose their fear of power
Then great power has indeed arrived.

Do not intrude on the people's material living.
Do not despise their spiritual lives, either.
If you respect them, you will be respected.

Therefore the Sage knows himself,
but he is not opinionated.
He loves himself, but he is not arrogant.

He lets go of conceit and opinion,
and embraces self-knowledge and love.

73

A soldier who has the courage to fight
will eventually be killed.
But one who has the courage not to fight will live.

In these two, one is good and the other harmful.
Who knows why Heaven allows some things to happen?
Even the Sage is stumped sometimes.

The Way of Heaven
Does not compete, but is good at winning;
Does not speak, yet always responds;
Does not demand, but is usually obeyed;
Seems chaotic, but unfolds a most excellent plan.

Heaven's net is cast wide
And though its meshes are loose,
Nothing is ever lost.

74

If people do not fear death
How can you threaten them with it?

If people live in constant fear of death,
Because those who break the law are seized and killed,
Who would dare to break the law?

There has always been an official executioner.
If you take the law into your own hands
And try to take his place,
It is like trying to take the place of a master carpenter
In which case you would probably hurt your hands.

75

The people are starving because their leaders
eat up all their money in taxes.
And so, they are hungry.

The people are rebellious
because their leaders are intrusive.
And so, they protest.

The people make light of death because their leaders
live so well at their expense.
And so, they expect death.

Therefore, it seems that one who does not grasp this life
too tightly is better off than one who clings.

76

When people are alive they are soft and weak.
At their death they are hard and rigid.

All young things, including grass and trees
Are soft and frail.
At their death they are withered and dry.

So, all that are hard and rigid take the company of death.
Those who are soft and weak take the company of life.

Therefore, powerful weapons will not succeed
(Remember that strong and tall trees
are the ones that are cut down).

The strong and rigid are broken and laid low.
The soft and weak will always overcome.

77

The Tao of Heaven is like the stringing of a bow.
The high is pressed down and the low is raised up.
The string that is too long is shortened
and the string that is too short is added to.

Heaven's Way is to take from what has too much
And give it to what does not have enough.
This is not the way of men, however,
for they take from those who have little
to increase the wealth of the rich.

So who is it that has too much
and offers it to a needy World?
Only someone who knows the Tao.

Therefore, the Sage works anonymously.
She achieves great things
but does not wait around for praise.
She does not want her talents to attract attention to her.

78

In the whole World nothing is softer or weaker than water.
And yet even those who succeed when attacking
the hard and the strong cannot overcome it
Because nothing can harm it.
The weak overcomes the strong.
The soft conquers the hard.

> No one in the World can deny this
> Yet no one seems to know how to put it into practice.

Therefore the Sage says
"One who accepts a people's shame is qualified to rule it.
One who embraces a condemned people
is called the king of the Universe."

> True words seem paradoxical.

79

When enemies are reconciled, some resentment invariably remains.
How can this be healed?

    Therefore the Sage makes good on his half of the deal
    And demands nothing of others.

    One who is truly good will keep his promise.
    One who is not good will take what he can.

    Heaven doesn't choose sides
    It is always with the good people.

80

It is best to have small communities with few people.
And although they have goods and equipment in abundance
few of them are even used.
They have great love of life,
and are content to be right where they are.
And although they have boats and carriages,
there is no place they particularly want to go.
And although they have access to weapons and machineries
of war, they have no desire to show them off.

> Let people return to simplicity,
> working with their own hands.
> Then they will find joy in their food
> Beauty in their simple clothes
> Peace in their living
> Fulfillment in their traditions.

And although they live within sight of neighboring states
And their roosters and dogs are heard by one another
The people are content to grow old and die
Without having gone to see their neighbor states.

81

True words are not beautiful.
Beautiful words are not true.

Good people do not argue.
Argumentative people are not good.

The wise are not necessarily well-educated.
The well-educated are not necessarily wise.

The Sage does not hoard things.
The more she does for others
The more she finds she has.
The more she gives to others
The more she finds she gains.

Heaven's Way is to nourish, not to harm.
The Sage's Way is to work, yet not compete.

1

The Nature of the Tao

THE FIRST question we must address is this: Is the Tao God? Obviously, there is no avoiding this question. It was certainly the question most present in my mind during my initial reading of the *Tao Te Ching*. So, in the spirit of the Tao, I will answer: yes and no. Before we can really answer this properly, we will need to examine some of the common ground between the Christian conception of God and the Tao.

The very first line of the *Tao Te Ching* says that the Tao cannot be described in words and then promptly proceeds to do just that. Still, we must give Lao Tzu credit for trying. For something that is cognitively incomprehensible and verbally impossible to render, he did a magnificent job. And it is typical of him, and Taoist tradition, to make contradictions at every opportunity, thereby illustrating that incomprehensibility. If we are to know it at all, it must be an intuitive, instinctual knowledge. An old Zen story says that a master may point the way, but we must be careful we are not just looking at his finger. Words are merely the finger and can never adequately encompass the infinitude of the Tao. Lao Tzu says, "The only thing you can say about the Tao, / is that it is elusive and evasive." This is typical of any discussion of God, or should be. Carl Jung wrote,

"Whenever we speak of religious contents we move in a world of images that point to something ineffable."[1] If there is one concept that most faith traditions share it is that God is beyond: beyond that which we experience, beyond our conceptual ability.

> Unintelligible to all understanding
> and immeasurable by all measure
> improportionable by every proportion
> and incomparable by all comparison
> infigurable by all figuration
> and unformable by all formation
> immovable by all motion
> and unimaginable by all imagination
> insensible to all sensation
> and intractable to all attraction
> untastable in all taste
> and inaudible in all hearing.
>
> —Nicholas of Cusa [2]

The point of all this is that no matter what tradition one is speaking from, at one point all traditions agree that God "transcends whatever they have the wit or even the grace to mean by the term."[3] Alarming as this may sound, what this means is that all possible conceptions of God are incomplete and insufficient, including both the Taoist and Christian conceptions. This will be hard to hear for some Christians, but it cannot be denied. Perhaps it is true that God chose to relate to humankind through the three personalities represented in the Trinity, but even that august doctrine is too small a vessel to contain Him. (In fact, the pronoun "Him" is thoughtless and inadequate, as we shall see.) If the Trinity in its wholeness is inadequate, then certainly any of the singular "persons" of the Trinity is more so. It is painfully obvious to the Christian that the Old Testament God is a different God from that revealed in the New Testament. And as for the Son, W.C. Smith says, "God is not revealed fully in Jesus Christ to me, nor indeed to anyone that I have met; or that my historical studies have uncovered."[4]

I have found helpful at this point a story often told in the East.

The story describes five blind men who have never beheld or been near to an elephant. Each approaches it from a different direction. One, feeling the trunk, says, "Ah! An elephant is just like a snake!" The second, feeling a leg, says, "Oh, elephants are just like tree trunks." A third, at the elephant's side, cries, "An elephant is a living wall!" A fourth, having in his hands an ear, commented, "Elephants are like fans." The fifth, feeling the tail, said, "Elephants are like thin strips of rope." All of these men are correct. Each portion of the elephant is as they describe. Their error, however, is that their individual portions are not the whole. No doubt they quarreled afterwards about their experience with the elephant. Perhaps they even launched crusades to prove by the sword who was correct. This is their, and our, folly; if they had shared their information, they would have come closer to the truth. No doubt it would still have been inadequate. They would not know, for instance, that the elephant is gray or that it is four-footed or how many eyes it has, but they would have been closer.

The lesson we can learn from this story is all too obvious. Yes, we can affirm that the Trinity is God, but it is not comprehensibly God. So, if like the blind men above, we could only sit down and discuss God as we have experienced God through our lives and traditions, we would perhaps have a much clearer, and a much more accurate picture.

What, then, can we learn from our brethren, the Taoists? How have they traditionally conceived of God? To understand the Tao from their perspective, we need first to look at a couple of aspects of Asian culture that give rise to it. I have a friend who spent some time in Thailand and China as a missionary, and I was fascinated by his observation that the smallest human unit is not, as in the West, the individual, but the family. There is no individual, only the units into which each person fits: world, nature, nation, tribe, corporation, and family. There is little of the existential angst, or alienation so familiar to us Westerners; in the East one is part of the whole. This is of course reflected in Eastern theology.

In the East, one is not separate from nor dominant over nature. One is a part of nature. The Taoist sees him or herself as equal to all other things in Creation and, in fact, it is from observing nature that wisdom is gleaned. Nature is correct. Humans think too much and that gets us into trouble. Nature, including humankind and the Tao, is a unit. Therefore, the Tao is a part of Nature, or more accurately, nature is a part of the Tao, and therefore the Tao is not a separate personality, like the Christian God. The Tao is impersonal. This sounds like a negative thing, and irreconcilable to the Christian conception of God, but it is in fact neither. *The Tao is God as nature sees God.* The sparrow, who cannot fall without God's knowledge (Matt. 10:29) does not have a "personal relationship" with God. The sparrow does not perceive God as a personality but as the very web of being in which it moves and of which it consists. The Taoist follows the example of the animals and the Earth herself, and perceives God in the same Way.

The Tao is not the Creator, for that assumes personality. Instead, the Tao is the source of creation. "The world has an origin," says Lao Tzu, "which we may regard as the Mother of the Universe." Creation is not shaped and labored over. Instead there was the Tao in labor, and the Universe was given birth to. This feminine attribute is quite appropriate for the Tao, for though it is truly the balance of feminine and masculine energies, its demeanor is primarily soft, gentle, and unobtrusive. "Know the active, the masculine, / Yet keep to the passive, the feminine." The feminine deity is common among native religions (Taoism is China's), and is quite a contrast to those of the masculine "sky gods" (which includes our own tradition). There is something about the feminine in deity which is powerfully attractive, to men as well as women. Women are thought of as being more forgiving, more compassionate than men, and we project these stereotypes onto our deities. There has always been a gaping void in Christian spirituality which only the feminine Divine could fill, a point well illustrated by many references in the Old Testament which image God in a feminine role.[5]

In the Church's first thirteen hundred years, this void was dealt with primarily by patriarchal repression and, more visibly, by the use of Christ as a surrogate goddess. Many of our historical renderings, including Eastern icons, picture Jesus as thin, weak, and actually effeminate. Eventually, women who became saints would help fill this role, culminating in the phenomenal rise of Mary to a position near that of Christ. This was in itself a salvation of sorts. The Christian patriarchy, so bent by the fear of woman, had convinced the known world that women were the seed of evil: Through Eve, evil entered the world and through her daughters evil is perpetuated. We might be able to pass this off as a perverse form of ecclesiastical sour grapes, but for women there was no cure and little comfort.

Mary was, in a very real, psychological way, the salvation of women. Through her, woman was no more merely the confederate of the serpent, but near to divinity herself. In her, women saw hope, and a reprieve from their intrinsic sinfulness before God. Mary liberated the captive women's spirit, only now finally coming to some semblance of completion. Mary continues to function as the archetypical goddess in Catholic spirituality. Protestants have rejected her out of hand with no comprehension of the danger of claiming a solely masculine deity, and no understanding of the true function of Mary as the feminine mask of the Christian God. The historical Mary has little to do with the deity apart from the myth of her origin. Within our own tradition, Mechtild of Magdeburg has written:

> God is not only fatherly.
> God is also mother
>   who lifts her loved child
>   from the ground to her knee.
> The Trinity is like a mother's cloak
> wherein the child finds a home
> and lays its head on the maternal breast.[6]

It is important to see the need human beings have for a compassionate deity, and a productive, or non-destructive, spirituality. In the last fifteen years many Protestant charismatic groups have begun referring to the Holy Spirit as feminine, some going as far as calling her goddess, and at least ascribing to her the feminine pronoun. This is a bit unsettling to the deeply orthodox, but we cannot ignore the historical resurgence, nor can we render it invalid as

Satan's deception. Satan's deception was keeping half of the human race in literal slavery without social, religious, or personal recognition, beaten back by a violently oppressive theology that reduced them to a subhuman, reproductive role.

When we rediscover the divine feminine, we are all—women and men—liberated. The angry sky-god becomes a vessel of nurture and compassion. It also serves to reinforce the feminine in the thinking and maturation of men, too. If God is not threatened by the feminine in Him/Herself, then we who are created in God's image also ought not be threatened.

I have often returned from discussions on gender to an imagination exercise which occurred to me after wrestling with these issues. Consider what would have happened if Ur of the Chaldees had been a matrifocal civilization; would it have been Sarah rather than Abraham who was called? And would God then be Goddess? And would Jesus have been born a woman? Would the Trinity be referred to as Mother, Daughter, and Holy Spirit? And what are the implications of this in the development of Christianity? It's a staggering experiment! Another experiment I tried was the use of feminine pronouns for God in my everyday life, consciously substituting "Her" for "Him" and "She" for "He." I did this for about a week, and both my wife and I were shaken up a bit. It is truly frightening how deep-seated our prejudices are.

Having established the Tao's divinity and androgyny, let us make a list of some of the Tao's other attributes:

> *It never refuses life to any being.*
> *It never demands recognition for its work.*
> *It does not demand allegiance.*
> *It makes no demands for itself.*
> *It does not claim to be great.*
> *It gives birth but does not possess.*
> *It acts, but takes no credit.*
> *It guides, but does not control.*

What can we say about these statements? They are totally selfless. The Tao is a remarkable deity because, much like Jesus in the

Gospels, it models what it teaches. It also goes against our desire for comfort, for recognition, and for gratitude. Lao Tzu calls this "the mystery of goodness." Jesus' ministry is the very picture of the Taoist sage. He never requested payment for his gifts of healing, nor did he seek recognition for his miracles. In fact he forbade most of those whom he helped to say anything about him. He owned little, if anything, having not even a place to sleep (Luke 9:58). And whereas the God of Israel promises that "Every valley shall be exalted, and every mountain and hill shall be made low" (Is. 40:4), the Tao likewise "blunts the sharp, / Unties the knotted, / Shades the bright" and, as "the Word was made flesh, and dwelt among us" (John 1:14) the Tao "unites with all Dust." This is indeed an awesome mystery, which we will consider in detail in a later chapter.

Another way in which the Tao resembles the Christian God is in its compassion and mercy. The Tao, Lao Tzu describes, is like the Universe's bosom upon which we can seek comfort and assurance. The Tao's love is unconditional. It is not there for the enlightened only, or the holy or necessarily the moral. The Tao is there for all. "It is the good person's treasure / And the bad person's refuge." It is not only for the pure of heart, either. I remember a sermon delivered in a small service just prior to communion. The pastor did not issue the typical precautions to partaking. In fact, he did not demand that we "confess up" and be right with God. "Jesus," he said, "is here for everyone. If your heart is troubled or if your sin is so great that you cannot stand to face it, that is all the more reason to come to the Lord's table. Jesus is here for you." "But if one's heart is not pure," writes Lao Tzu, "that is all the more reason to cling to the Tao!" And we continue to hear the echo of the Gospel when he asks, "Why did the Sages of old value the Tao so much? / Because, when you seek, you find / And when you sin, you are forgiven." As with Christ, no one is keeping score of our successes and failures. Like Jesus, "Its essence is unquestionably genuine. / You can put your faith in it."

The *Tao Te Ching* makes great use of opposites, as we shall see in the next chapter. One of the most important sets of opposites is "existence" and "non-existence." Without jumping ahead too much, "existence" usually can be thought of as that which is contained in the material world, while "non-existence," "emptiness," or "nothing-ness" usually refers to what we would call spiritual realities. So when we hear Lao Tzu telling us that the "Tao is like an empty pitcher, / Poured from, but never drained," we can imagine that what is poured from this pitcher is "living water" which "will become in him a spring of water welling up to eternal life" after which one will "never thirst" again (John 4:10-11).

This emptiness is never exhausted, and the more one draws on it the more it produces. It does not make a show to get our attention. And even though it is the most obvious force in the Universe, display-ing itself in all it gives birth to, it does not demand our recognition or even care if it is noticed. It is just there. When we begin to notice these things, we start to discover who we really are, as Jesus did during his forty days in the wilderness. Through studying the Tao, we become sensitive to vast new aspects of God's working in the natural world which we have been blind to. We also have a greater understanding of what it means to be both creature and image of the Creator.

Thomas Merton wrote,

> How absolutely central is the truth that we are first of all part of nature, though we are a very special part, that which is conscious of God. In solitude, one is entirely surrounded by beings which perfectly obey God. This leaves only one place open for me, and if I occupy that place then I, too, am fulfill-ing God's will. The place nature "leaves open" belongs to the conscious one, the one who is aware, who sees all this as a unity, who offers it all to God in praise, joy, thanks. To me, these are not "spiritual acts" or special virtues, but rather the simple, normal, obvious functions of humankind, without which it is hard to see how one can be human . . .[7]

2

Paradox

I T is the rule in religious studies that truth is inexplicably bound up in paradox. "True words seem paradoxical," says Lao Tzu, and the principle seems to be fairly universal. Fundamentalists, in fact, may say that it is paradoxical that a glimmer of God's truth can possibly emerge from within other, "pagan" religions. But emerge it does, beyond all comprehension. Paradox—the union of opposites— is one of the great themes of Taoist thought.

The symbol of the Tao looks like two tadpoles, one white, one black, chasing each others' tails. The white tadpole has a black dot, like an eye, and the black, a white eye. This simple image, when dwelt upon, can teach us more about the Tao (and thereby nature) than any number of volumes on the subject. The white one is called yin, and the black one, yang. Separate them and you really have nothing but tadpoles, but together they make an image of eternity, a circle, a whole, the Tao. They represent the concept of opposites which are dependent upon each other for their being.

> The Tao gives birth to one.
> One gives birth to two.
> Two gives birth to three,
> And three gives birth to all things.

This verse is admittedly cryptic, but it is not impenetrable. The "One" of line one is the primal Tao, unrefracted, pre-distinctive; perhaps what scientists like Stephen Hawking would call a singularity. This singularity divides itself (*by* itself) into the "two" of line two. The result of this mitosis is equal and opposite halves, the Yin, and Yang. Now, as the result of some seeming sleight-of-hand, the two instantaneously create the third: the Whole. Now there is the Yang, the Yin, and the Tao (the union of Yin and Yang). One way of illustrating this is by looking at a marriage. A marriage consists of three people, not two. There is the person of the man, the person of the woman, and a separate but equal person of the relationship. This unseen third person is often the One to which both the man and the woman devote most of their energy, for it is only through the third person that they have their union.

A similar case can be made for the Trinity, the Holy Spirit being the one who "proceeds from the Father and the Son." Now, regardless of what the Yang and Yin do or become, the Tao presides and balances all. In fact, Lao Tzu wants to take us beyond the union of opposites, until we forget that they even *are* opposites. "[One who is full of goodness] does not recognize the union of male and female / For she knows it as an undivided whole." There is a haunting portrait of this in the crucifixion, suggested by John S. Dunne, in which we see the "good" thief hanging to the right of Jesus, and the "bad" thief crucified to his left. In this one scene we see "the image of the Crucified [Christ] as the mysterious 'third' or uniting symbol 'between' good and evil." [1]

It would not be wise to continue without some clarification of the symbology of Yin and Yang. Yang is "force." It is active, while Yin is "acquiescence" and passive. Yang is "light," whereas Yin is the absence of light, or "dark." Yang is "warm" and "friendly," Yin, "cool" and "shy." Yang is "masculine" and corresponds to the sky, while Yin is "feminine" and takes to the Earth.

Many of my students are initially confused. They expect Yang to be dark and Yin, light, and want to contribute "evil" to Yang and "good" to Yin. But neither Yang nor Yin is evil. Yang and Yin simply are, and too much of either may prove to be troublesome. This is a much more slippery concept than the simplistic one the students initially assume.

Lao Tzu clearly loved paradox and a good portion of his book is devoted to its subtleties: a larger percentage, in fact, than any other single topic he addresses. Why is this? Because it is central to life and therefore central to the Tao. Let's look at some of them:

> *True perfection seems flawed.*
> *True fulfillment seems empty.*
> *True straightness seems crooked.*
> *Great skill appears easy.*
> *Great eloquence sounds awkward.*
> *The path into light seems dark.*
> *The way ahead seems to go backwards.*
> *The path into peace seems rough.*
> *True purity seems stained.*
> *Appropriate caution seems like cowardice.*

Don't most of these ring true to us? Can't we think of at least one example for each of the above; in the Gospels or in the life of great prophets such as Martin Luther King, Jr. or Mahatma Gandhi? Don't we recognize these truths from the experience of our own lives? The question remains, though, *why* is it this way? Why should truth be so bound up in paradox?

Truth does not exist in a vacuum. Truth is only true in how it relates to our experience. Truth, then, has a relationship with reality and with its opposite, falsehood. This is the point at which the Tao can help us out. The Taoist believes that at the extreme of Yin, Yang appears, and at the extreme of Yang, Yin appears. Just look at the Tao symbol to see that where Yang is greatest, Yin begins and vice versa. They have a relationship, as do all opposites. A concrete example would be a feverish child. You want to break the fever so that his temperature will go back to normal, so what do you do? You do not pour cool water over him; instead you pile on the blankets so that he sweats and sweats until, finally, the fever breaks and he cools down. Why was it necessary to make him warmer? Why did that work, when cool water would not? Because at the extreme of Yang (heat), Yin (coolness) begins. This is attested to over and over in Chinese medicine; it is one of its central tenets. So ask St. John of the Cross about "the path into light" being the "Dark Night of the Soul." Ask anyone who has wrestled with their conscience about "the way ahead" seeming to go backwards. Only by *breaking through* is real progress made, and therefore we must not despise the rough, the dark, the empty, the cowardly, the flawed, or the crooked. It is a package deal. These must also be embraced, for without them their opposites cannot exist. The *relationship* must be bought as a unit or not at all. Lao Tzu explains this in the second chapter:

> When people see beauty as beautiful,
> They recognize other things as ugly.
> When people see goodness as good,
> They recognize other things as being bad.
> Therefore existence and non-existence produce one another
> Difficult and easy achieve each other
> Long and short define each other
> High and low rely on each other
> Voice and accompaniment harmonize with one another
> Front and back follow each other.

The greatest problem posed to theologians of all time is the very existence of evil. Yet without evil there would be no good. If there were no suffering, we would not appreciate grace even if it leaped up and bit our noses. Life would have all the savor of unprepared tofu and would hardly be worth our time and trouble. Truth is not found in good in isolation, but only in good as it relates to its opposite. The point is that neither good nor evil is important; what is important *is the tension between the two* as they relate to our own particular situations. As William Dols writes, "The meaning and message is discovered not by . . . resolving the dilemma, but when such contradictory truths are held in tension and new meaning emerges at a third point . . . 'the intersection of the incompatibles.'"[2] Nicholas of Cusa calls Divinity "the coincidence of opposites."[3] Lao Tzu would call it the Tao. There is no other way to reconcile such enigmas, nor to eliminate dualism. Dualism, according to Lao Tzu, is an illusion that has kept the people in confusion for a very long time. We should also keep in mind the difficulty we humans have in distinguishing good and evil. We certainly have some understanding and must do our best to be discerning, but our discernment must also contain a grain of humility for our time-bound mortal limitations. As Carrin Dunne explains,

> We call something good or evil within the context of a particular situation as we perceive it. There are two qualifiers at work here: the time frame and our understanding of what is good or bad for us. We do not have the "big picture," a total view of history, so what may appear to be evil in the short run may turn out to be a greater good in the long run. Also, we have a limited understanding of what is best for us. . . . Evil is part of the Mystery.[4]

The classic dualistic debate is about the relationship between body and spirit. In the *Tao Te Ching,* we are asked, "Being both body and spirit, / can you embrace unity and not be fragmented?" The true human being does not reside in the spirit, nor is the human really only animal; he or she is neither one nor the other, but both, the tension found between the opposites. Lao Tzu asks a very difficult question above, one with which humankind has struggled from its earliest philosophical records. Every culture perceives this dualistic nature of the human, but not all of them deal with it in the same way. The Western way has been predominantly dualistic, while the Eastern has been traditionally unitive. Is there a right or a wrong view? If we set as our standard the Biblical discernment "by their fruits you shall know them," perhaps it is possible to tell. Our earliest philo-sophical forebears, the Jews, were primarily unitive. As stated above, the future spiritual life was irrelevant to the present physical situa-tion. The Jews were spiritually and physically well integrated. The spiritual being was not separate from the physical being. Physical action carried spiritual import, and vice versa. But when we look at the next major philosophical contributors, the Greeks, our trouble begins. The dualism in this philosophy was not of a good/evil variety, but of an insubstantial/substantial sort. Only the world of ideas or spiritual realities mattered. The physical world was transient and illusory, and could therefore be regarded as having little import.

The Mystery religions from the first couple of centuries provided a means for believers to pierce the veil of seeming reality and enjoy communion with the wholly spiritual through symbolic ritual acts. (This is sort of ironic, since once again physical means are employed to effect spiritual realities.) When Christianity was sweeping over the "Greek" world, a dualistic heresy, Gnosticism, emerged, which taught that, once again, matter and spirit are separate and not rec-oncilable. Gnosticism believed that the spiritual world was pure and eternal, while physical reality was, again, transient and irredeemably evil. Jesus, the Gnostics taught, only *seemed* to have flesh and hu-man form, for since he (in the Gnostic mythos) is high in the spiri-tual hierarchy, he could not possibly have contact with the evil material world. Grace only travels downward from the most pure, most holy beings, through a descending number of progressively less spiritual and more material demiurges and messengers until, at the bottom of the spiritual ladder, humankind is reached. (There was, in fact, one Gnostic sect which taught that although Jesus could urinate, He could not defecate!)[5] The early Church wrestled mightily with Gnostic ideas, as some congregations were so influenced that they believed their spirits to be incorruptible and it was therefore unimportant what they did with their bodies. Partly through this, and partly through St. Paul's own Greek-influenced theological vi-sion, Christianity was not spared the impact of Gnostic heresy. Paul taught that "in my flesh dwelleth no good thing" (Rom. 7:18); "the flesh lusteth against the Spirit, and the Spirit against the flesh." (Gal.

5:17) The effects of such spirit-body dualism have been disastrous, as evidenced by such "spiritual" practices as mortifying the flesh, ritual murder to redeem the spirit of heretics by the Holy Inquisition, the wanton destruction of Creation, and the often fatal psychological oppression by legalistic dogmatists of many Christian groups.

The *Tao Te Ching* speaks of matter and spirit as sort of partners, each of which is incapable of functioning without the other. As I stated earlier, Taoists speak of spirit as "non-existence," implying something that exists in objective reality, but which possess no physical manifestation, or "existence." Synonyms for spirit / "non-existence" are emptiness and non-being. Meister Eckhart in our own Christian tradition spoke in similar terms when he said that "God is a being beyond being and a nothingness beyond being."[6]

Lao Tzu presents non-being as absolutely necessary for physical realities to "function," and vice versa.

> Thirty spokes join together at one hub
> But it is the hole in the center that makes it operable.
> Clay is molded into a pot,
> But it is the emptiness inside that makes it useful.
> Doors and windows are cut to make a room,
> It is the empty spaces that we use.

The first time I read these verses, chills ran down my spine. I felt that I had been told a great secret that was in fact the most obvious thing in the world. That was the relationship between matter and spirit. One is not dominant. "Existence and non-existence produce one another." Lao Tzu finishes by explaining, "Existence is what we have, / But non-existence is what we use." Spirit is what animates these lifeless lumps of clay! Spirit has no expression on this planet without its lover, flesh. Spirit and flesh entwine in passionate embrace, loving one another, cherishing the gift the other brings! Scripture tells us that God looked on what He made and said, "It is very good." (Gen. 1:31) Nothing has happened to change that. Perhaps humankind's "fall" is partly a result of our forgetting just how "very good" it is. Matthew Fox suggests that the Original Sin is this very dualism itself.[7] We need to dig deep into our tradition and retrieve the wisdom that "the soul loves the body"[8] and celebrate it.

The last paradox we should address in this chapter is evidence of the Creator's great humor and Lao Tzu's sense of irony in noticing it. It is this: "The softest thing in the World overcomes the hardest thing in the World." It sounds simple, but how profound! It is one of the most important laws of the Universe.

> In the whole World nothing is softer or weaker than water.
> And yet even those who succeed when attacking
> the hard and the strong cannot overcome it
> Because nothing can harm it.
> The weak overcomes the strong.
> The soft conquers the hard.
> No one in the World can deny this
> Yet no one seems to know how to put it into practice.

Water's way of meeting force is by yielding. Yet, yielding, it is able to carve millions of miles of caverns out of solid rock. Water is responsible for the glories of the Grand Canyon and the Arizona mesas. Water, by yielding, by patience, has no enemy of equal. Rock it hews and metal it rusts, yet at the same time ministering to the needs of all living beings. This is the way of the Tao. As long as there is the Tao there will always be a David to defeat Goliath, a timid and victorious Gideon, an Esther with all her craft and gentility. This law was not lost on Jesus, a quiet man whose gentle integrity saw him murdered and ultimately the victor in his glorious resurrection. The yielding yet resolute Gandhi had learned this lesson, too, as had Martin Luther King, Jr. Their commitment to non-violence, to yielding, to gentility, are testament to this fundamental law: "To foster gentleness is true strength." Power is not determined, as man supposes, by the number of missiles stockpiled, the ratio of horses to footsoldiers, the number or ferocity of warriors, or the statistics of corporate clout. The victory will go to the one who knows how to yield.

3

Desire

THIS chapter hits a sore spot in so-called first-world societies, and industrialized societies particularly. We are a compulsive people, and knowing this, out of further compulsion, we exploit this flaw to the fullest in myriad advertisements, so commonplace that we often don't even notice them. Subconsciously, however, it serves only to fuel the fire of our desire. Lao Tzu summed up this situation when he said, "Too many colors tax people's vision. / Too many sounds deaden people's hearing. / Too many flavors spoil people's taste."

We live in a society that has become a malevolent carnival where the insatiable prey on the insatiable using every sensational contrivance imaginable. And we are numb to it. Do modern humans seem distant? Emotionless? The ideal lifestyles forced upon us make our daily existences seem dull affairs by comparison, leaving us with an evasive longing for that life that we "should" have, the life filled with adventure and romance and wealth that we see mocking us from every billboard, film, and television show. We feel that we are somehow "missing out," and as a result we don't recognize the beautiful and the small that are our real treasures. Instead we save and save and take lavish vacations trying to capture that ever-evasive adventure which we think we want so badly. We gamble—with money, our lives, and the affections of others—with as little regard for human feelings as a throw of the dice. "Thrill-seeking leads people to do crazy things," Lao Tzu says. Our lives are apparently so safe and dull that we must court death regularly to make life seem worth living: auto racing, suicide ski runs, bungee jumping, war games, big game hunting, and so on. Is our existence really so impoverished? What is this compulsion that drives at every one of us to risk, to gain, to possess?

In Eastern thought, the culprit is "desire" itself. Desire is the source of misery. To desire what one does not have betrays us, making it difficult to be grateful or celebrate what we do have. Desire short-circuits our happiness, our spirituality, and our relationships to our own health, to others around us, and to the Earth. Lao Tzu meets this situation head on and asks us some very difficult questions:

Fame or self: which is more important?

Your possessions or your person: which is worth more to you?

Gain or loss: which is worse?

Therefore, to be obsessed with "things" is a great waste,

The more you gain, the greater your loss.

You may fill your halls with gold and jewels
but you cannot keep them safe.

These are not new ideas to us. Jesus said,

> Do not store up for yourselves treasures on earth, where moth and rust destroy, and where thieves break in and steal. But store up for yourselves treasures in heaven, where moth and rust do not destroy, and where thieves do not break in and steal. For where your treasure is, there your heart will be also.
>
> (Matt. 6:19-21)

Jesus told us we must die to ourselves and our desires if we were ever going to find life in Him. "For whoever wants to save his life will lose it, but whoever loses his life for me will find it." (Matt. 16:25) To desire "things," or treasures on Earth, invariably leads to spiritual depravity. One of our great Christian mystics, St. John of the Cross, points out that "In clinging to things and accomplishments one becomes unhappy with self, cold toward neighbors, sluggish and slothful in the things of God."[1] Not only does desiring cause us (and those we touch) to suffer, but when we possess what we formerly desired, we are seldom happier; the focus of our desire simply shifts to something else. As Dante expresses it,

> Just as we see little children intensely longing for an apple, and then going on further longing for a little bird, and further on desiring fine clothes, and later a horse and then a lover, we perceive that the human soul never finds what she is ever searching for: the supreme good, God.[2]

We are possessed of a gnawing hunger for the Eternal that can never be adequately filled by anything temporal. Yet some people have perverted their search for the Eternal into the pursuit of more wealth. The "name it and claim it" brand of Protestant Evangelicalism is a prime example. They have just turned the situation inside out, but to an even more bitter end, by implicating God as a conspirator for their greed. This is by no means a purely modern phenomenon, however. Meister Eckhart several hundred years ago said,

> Some people, I swear, want to love God in the same way as they love a cow. They love it for its milk and cheese and the profit they will derive from it. Those who love God for the sake of outward riches or for the sake of inward consolation operate on the same principle. They are not loving God correctly; they are merely loving their own advantage.[3]

Greed is not limited to certain aspects of our lives, but corrupts even our faith practices. What solution can we find for this ancient disease? When the rich young ruler asked Jesus what to do to gain eternal life (more greed!), Jesus finally told him to "Sell everything you have and give to the poor, and you will have treasure in Heaven. Then come, follow me." (Luke 18:22) What was Jesus getting at? He was talking about a process called "emptying."

> There, where clinging to things ends, is where God begins to be. If a cask is to contain wine, you must first pour out the water. The cask must be bare and empty. Therefore, if you wish to receive divine joy and God, first pour out your clinging to things. Everything that is to receive must and ought to be empty.[4]

The quote above by Meister Eckhart echoes the words of Lao Tzu, "If you can empty yourself of everything, / you will have lasting peace." Both of these faith traditions take the issue very seriously. Some of Jesus' most difficult words are about this very thing. "Any of you who does not give up everything he has cannot be my disciple." (Luke 14:33) The elimination of attachments, and the focus of our energies elsewhere is the first step. Lao Tzu asks us, "When Heaven gives and takes away, / can you be content to just let things come or go?" The process of emptying is not complete unless, like Job, we can answer, "Naked I came from my mother's womb, and naked I will depart. The Lord gave and the Lord has taken away; may the name of the Lord be praised."(Job 1:21) It is true that Job's response to his losses is positively superhuman. Most of us are incapable of such detachment, but it is this very detachment that most Eastern traditions insist upon. When the Chinese army invaded Tibet and forced the Dalai Lama and the monks into exile, they did not curse the Chinese. Their detachment is so complete that even such drastic loss rarely disturbs their contentment.

If we feel that such utter detachment is impossible for everyday people, I am inclined to agree. Few of us possess such spiritual discipline that we can, like St. Francis, literally leave our former lives naked and rely on God alone for our nourishment. So what is God asking us to do? Simply to be content with what we have. Lao Tzu tells us, "There is no greater curse than discontent. / Nothing breeds trouble like greed. / Only one who is content with enough / will be content always." Is it possible in our maddening culture to be "content with enough?" The Tao, or God-in-nature always provides "enough." Jesus says, "Do not worry about your life, what you will eat; or about your body, what you will wear. Life is more than food and the body more than clothes." (Luke 12:22-3) These words of Jesus sound as alien to most Westerners' ears as any of the cryptic passages of Lao Tzu. It is precisely the antithesis of the way we live and the values we espouse.

So where do we turn? Lao Tzu gives us many examples of where not to turn: "Forget 'holiness,' abandon 'intelligence' / and people will be a hundred times better off." The legal code of the Pharisees and fundamentalists will not work. Humanly ordained laws are often made to be broken. Any legal system based on fear will prove an inadequate motivation for true "emptying"; it will make contentment impossible. Likewise knowledge alone is doomed to failure as well. God is experiential and spirituality is not a purely intellectual pursuit. The Tao "unites with all Dust" and is experienced through pain, ecstasy, and sweat. A faith that is not existential will not provide the discipline capable of emptying or sacrifice.

"Give up 'humanitarianism,' put away 'righteousness' / and people will rediscover brotherly love and kindness." Humanitarianism appeals to justice, and love is not simply just. Sacrifice for others does not necessarily occur out of a sense of justice, but is often a sacrifice of justice for the good of another. And righteousness is a kind of pride; paradoxically, once one is aware of one's own righteousness, he or she is guilty of pride and therefore no longer righteous.

"Forget 'great art,' throw away 'profit' / and there will be no more thieves." Great art assumes that one person's art is valuable and another's is worthless. If art were celebrated for the sake of personal expression, all art would be valuable, and no one would have to steal any, for they would simply make their own which would be infinitely more meaningful to them. Profit assumes that another suffers loss. When we game for profit, we game for more than "enough"; such a game quickly spirals out of control of the will and inevitably succumbs to greed.

"These things are superficial and are simply not enough," Lao Tzu teaches us, "People need something more solid to hold on to; and here it is:

Be real.
Embrace simplicity.
Put others first.
Desire little."

Such behavior, rare in our society, is precisely what the Gospel demands of us if we are honest with God and with ourselves.

Have you ever known someone who was really genuine? Such people are a breath of fresh air. I am captivated by them, and inspired by their fearless honesty. They have nothing to hide and so they have no reason to fear exposure. Even when this person's past is less than exemplary, they are up front about that, too, and possess a knowledge of forgiveness which renders the shame of the past impotent. They truly "embrace simplicity" in that they needn't construct excuses to explain their sins, nor to justify themselves to others. When they say something, you believe them. They know what it means to sacrifice and find joy in putting others' needs ahead of their own. Whence comes their strength?

When Dante meets the soul of Piccarda on the moon in the *Paradisio*, she tells him, "The power of Love quiets our wills and makes us wish only for what we have. We thirst for nothing else." [5] Love is certainly too nebulous a concept to offer as the cure-all for everything. But love-in-action is not. When Jesus commanded us to heal the sick, feed the hungry, give drink to the thirsty, shelter to the stranger, clothes to the naked, and company to the lonely (Matt. 25:34-6), he removes love from the conceptual realm and places it in front of our noses every day. It is "Love made flesh" in which God specializes, having little interest in whatever isn't united "with all Dust."

When Lao Tzu observes himself, he feels very out of place in a world where desire is a god.

Ordinary people are bright.
I alone seem dim.
Ordinary people are discriminating.
I alone am ambivalent.

As quiet as the ocean.
As free as the wind.

People rush about on their very important business.
But I alone seem incorrigible and uncouth.
I am different from ordinary people;
I enjoy feeding from the Great Mother's breasts.

Like Lao Tzu, we are called by love into a very different sort of life; one that is motivated by compassion rather than greed. We are called to feed "from the Great Mother's breasts," unconcerned about our next meal, trusting God to provide.

4

Non-Action

I N Non-action we find one of the most easily misunderstood concepts of Taoism. To Westerners—especially Americans—a line like, "When you practice 'not-doing,' nothing is left undone" sounds like a rationalization for supreme laziness. In fact it is just the opposite. Non-action is the most efficient means of accomplishing that there is, and for this reason it deserves our attention. This is so not because it is an exotic and interesting notion, but because most of us run the rat race as fast as we can, and suffer equally the damage caused by ulcers, heart attacks, nervous disorders, and general stress. Non-action is, in a way, a means to a fresh start, a new outlook, a more compassionate way of living towards others and ourselves.

The Chinese word for inaction is *wu-wei*. Wu-wei literally means "not doing," but it has many applications. It also means "not forcing" and that is the meaning which we will address first.

Wu-Wei

Using wu-wei begins with an understanding of The Way Things Are, as the Taoist sees it. The Taoist watches nature and sees that all that nature does—eroding mountains, growing forests, making rivers, birthing cubs—all this is accomplished effortlessly. Being one with the Tao, nature goes its own way and forces nothing; and yet grand works and great beauty result. Wu-wei, therefore, isn't inactive at all, but is activity at its most efficient, because it accomplishes without effort. When the sage, recognizing oneness with the Tao, acts upon his or her environment in the spirit of the Tao, then, as Thomas Merton writes,

> His [or her] action is not a violent manipulation of exterior reality, an "attack" on the outside world, bending it to his conquering will: on the contrary, he respects external reality by yielding to it . . . a perfect accomplishment of what is demanded by the precise situation.[1]

This intuitive form of action plays itself out in the natural world, the interpersonal world, and the personal inner world. Benjamin Hoff in *The Tao of Pooh* (a wonderful introduction to Taoism through the stories of Winnie-the-Pooh), believes that it "seems rather significant that the character *Wei* developed from the symbols for a clawing hand and a monkey, since the term *wu-wei* means not going against the nature of things; no clever tampering; no Monkeying Around."[2] Like everything else in nature, humankind should live effortlessly. This means working hard, as the beaver does, but not going against Nature's grain, as we humans tend to want to do at every opportunity. Then our work pours out of us in a spirit of joy and fulfillment—not, as is often the case, work being a curse which we must somehow endure daily from nine to five.

Not Forcing: The Will

"A truly good person does not try to be good, / Therefore is he able to be good. / Another ordinary person tries to be good, / and finds that he cannot." Most of us are ordinary persons—myself included—but that is no reason to despair. For one thing, anyone who has wrestled with their own guilt will recognize the truth of this statement. No matter how firm our resolve, how deep our commitment, we cannot seem to maintain anything remotely resembling a perfect state. "Whoever tries will fail," says Lao Tzu, for once again we are *forcing* nature, not flowing along with it. Any time we resort to forcing, we are destined to failure. The reasons for this differ with the situation, but at the root *going contrary to nature* is always the cause. In the case of righteousness, any effort will only result in failure, if only because the moment we think we are actually being righteous, we succumb to the sin of pride. And such trying will certainly not bring us closer to the Tao.

What is the solution, then? Not to *try*. This is, of course, impossible, but this should not deter us, since in the Tao impossible things are the norm, not the exception. "Therefore the Sage, not trying, cannot fail / Not clutching, she cannot lose." Remember that "A truly good person does not try to be good." Goodness needs to come naturally, effortlessly, like breathing or hearing. The Sage is not concerned with being good. This is very important. He or she does not give it a thought. It is not a goal. The goal is to respond humanely—as a human would—to whatever situation life gives. If the natural response to an event is anger, the Sage does not question the feelings rising up within; he or she just lives in them. If the natural response is joy, they will most likely smile, but they will not think, "Why am I smiling? Is it really appropriate to smile? Perhaps I shouldn't look so happy because I might make other people feel bad by comparison . . ." and so on. The Sage will just smile, and not waste energy on analysis.

Neither will the Sage waste time mourning over past mistakes. He or she knows that "when you sin, you are forgiven," and does not dwell on it. He or she simply returns to the natural flow of the Tao. Sensitive Christians (and this is speaking from *personal* experience) expend so much energy in guilt and remorse over trivial legalistic non-issues that they undermine all of God's gifts and blessings. They live in hopelessness and a feeling of moral failure so deep that they cannot (in some cases will not) let go of their own sins, even though God has long ago "let go" of them. In fact, "to let go" is the literal meaning of the word for "forgiveness" in New Testament Greek. This inability to "let go" and forgive oneself turns the Gospel into "bad news," a means of self-oppression which is only amplified by futile attempts at outward piety. This is tragic. God would much rather we "let go" of all those things and notice the crickets chirping outside or the way the cat's eyes move when it's dreaming. This is called "being present," and it is an essential part of living in the Tao. Living righteously will come naturally when you don't try—if you don't try you can't fail! We need but to immerse ourselves in the wonder of Creation, of the Tao, and not waste any more time with this guilt foolishness.

What happens when we do this? We find that we are acting "from the heart." We are living as we were meant by God to live. Lao Tzu adds that the "politician acts, but he has ulterior motives." The politician acts out of an interest for him/herself. In this way, most of us are politicians, vying for the "righteousness" vote from our churchmates, the "popularity" vote from our co-workers and friends. This is not genuine living. This is living out of insecurity, out of a deficient self-image. But "When a legalist acts and gets no response, / He rolls up his sleeves and uses force." This is a good description of oppressive, self-defeating religion which causes no end of destruction. It is also a good description of many other oppressive structures, from the military to the private business sector.

Not Forcing: Physical

From the example of the legalist above, it is implied that forcing the will leads to physical force. The Taoist has nothing against physical action in itself, but rather, as Holmes Welch describes, "all hostile, aggressive action. Many kinds of action are innocent. Eating and drinking, making love, plowing a wheatfield, running a lathe—these may be aggressive acts, but generally they are not."[3]

The Taoist finds that there are humane and reliable methods to achieve one's end. It is easier to direct the growth of a young sapling than a giant redwood. It is the nature of a sapling to be flexible and therefore easily influenced by its environment, including us. But to direct a mature redwood is another matter altogether. This would without question be forcing the tree against its nature and would probably destroy the tree. Therefore the Taoist says,

Deal with the difficult while it is still easy.
Begin great works while they are small.

A tree too big around to hug is produced from a tiny sprout.
A nine-story tower begins with a mound of dirt.
A thousand-mile journey begins with your own two feet.

The distinction here is between influence and aggression. Ideally, influence is the path that the Christian should pursue as well. One should not force one's body to leap unprepared into a twenty kilometer marathon; one should influence one's body slowly, so that it gradually becomes sufficiently conditioned for such things. Not to do so would not only be violent, but would demonstrate a profound lack of compassion for the self.

Many people see in Lao Tzu's "Repay hatred with kindness" a parallel with Jesus' command to "turn the other cheek." It is a fitting comparison, yet it is all the more interesting when we discover that, yes, the commands are similar, the actions described are similar, but the motivations are quite different. For Christians, "turn the other cheek" is something motivated both by our love for God and for our fellow human beings. The Taoist motivation is not nearly so philanthropic. For the Taoist, one should "repay hatred with kindness" because it is a method that works. It is the best way to achieve our desired results. It is purely functional. These divergent viewpoints offer a gift to both Christians and Taoists that we can share: For the Taoist, such behavior is a sacrifice that demonstrates the individual's devotion; and for the Christian there is the comfort that in following Jesus' command, we have a most effective—and humane—means of accomplishing our goals in the face of the most hostile opposition.

Not-Doing

Not-doing is the most delightful interpretation of non-action. It is also very difficult for Westerners to accomplish consciously, and yet it happens to us all the time. This process values *being* over *doing*. It involves being completely absorbed in one's activity, with full attention and skills brought to bear in the present moment to the effect that there is no division between oneself and one's work. For instance, suppose I am washing dishes (not one of my favorite activities). If, while washing, I am thinking, "I can't wait to get this over with . . . what should I wear tonight? . . . I've got to make time to study that report . . . thank God this is the last fork . . . I *hate* forks . . ." etc., I am obviously not engrossed in my activity, I am off in fantasyland, actively hating this chore. This is not my idea of a good time.

The Taoist, on the other hand, would consider such activity an excellent opportunity for meditative practice. The goal would be to focus the mind solely on what one is doing, not day-dreaming, consciously returning the mind to one's work when one realizes it has strayed. When I am successful at this, I enter totally into the experience, I am fully present, aware of all that my senses bring me, engrossed in the activity. I stop "doing" the dishes, and start "being" the act of doing the dishes. This is difficult to express in words, but the concept is pretty simple: instead of "doing" work, I become the work. I am the work. And so it is no longer work; it is being fully present in the "Eternal Now," a state of grace where I am fully conscious of my own presence and the presence of God. The work, no matter how trivial, is an expression, a celebration of being alive. Doing the dishes has never been the same! Not that I am able to achieve this state regularly—I am a bit of a worry-wart. But when it does happen, it's magic. I found that it has occurred most often when I have worked, during my high-school and college years, as a retail cashier. At a restaurant, a bowling alley, or a record shop, whenever we were "swamped," simply too busy to think of anything but moving on to the next customer, these were places that I "became" my work most easily. Time then dashes by, for I am at one with my activity. I am being, not doing.

As Lao Tzu said, "Close your mouth / Go easy on the senses / And life will not be so hard," because your activities will cease to be empty toil. Mechtild of Magdeburg said, "The noblest joy of the senses, the holiest peace of the heart, the most resplendent luster of all good works derives from this: That the creature puts his or her heart wholly into what he or she does."[4] I am reminded that Brother Lawrence, one of our medieval Christian mystics, who wrote the classic *The Practice of the Presence of God*, was a mere cook and dishwasher in his monastery, and his advice is very similar.

When one is able to accomplish this state of "being," one experiences a contentment that goes beyond material pleasure. We may be surprised that, in this absence of desiring, one actually tastes contentment; and this could conceivably be a cause for great discomfort, because it directly challenges our materialistic conditioning. Thomas Merton wrote: "The whole thing boils down to giving ourselves in prayer a chance to realize that we have what we seek. We don't have to rush after it. It is there all the time, and if we give it time, it will make itself known to us."[5] God is always and everywhere present and it is our great good fortune to recognize this in anything we do.

Not-doing also implies the most obvious activity of having no activity. That the act of bathing in the sun should be a holy activity may seem to our work-prone ears a ludicrous idea. We conveniently neglect scripture that admonishes us to be still before the Lord. (Ps. 46:10) Lao Tzu tells us, "If you spend your life filling your senses / And rushing around 'doing' things / You will be beyond hope." It is difficult for some of us to slow down and not to feel guilty. This is self-destructive behavior, as spiritually detrimental as it is physically debilitating. To rest, to "waste" time is opportunity for contemplation and centering. There are monastic communities that are engaged in no other activities but contemplation of God's creation and being still.

I myself have always had trouble understanding how some people can "loaf around" and not feel worthless and lazy. Yet some have the gift. I, and many like me, take life much too seriously, and in that we miss the very point of life itself. Alan Watts writes,

> Children (and adults who have their wisdom) are usually the most happy when they are doing things that have no particular purpose—making up lunatic stories with friends, walking aimlessly through fields and hitting at old stumps with a stick, whittling hunks of wood just for the sake of whittling and drawing wayward and interminable designs on scraps of paper.
>
> There is a timeless and peaceful satisfaction in these actions, a fascination such that it would seem possible to go on with them for all eternity. To sit and watch the changing shapes of clouds, or specks of dust floating in the sunlight,

or the patterns of concentric circles made in a pool by the falling rain—the contemplative happiness of these things belongs to that childlike wisdom which must be learned again before one may enter the kingdom of heaven, for the reason, it must be, that the activity of heaven is of a similar kind.[6]

Most people are familiar with St. Francis' habit of preaching to the animals, and many would call him mad. But it may be that he was merely returning the favor of nature's ministry to him. Jesus found much wisdom in God's creation, and often used the flower or an animal to illustrate a truth about the kingdom of heaven. Creation itself is an invaluable source of wisdom, for insight into ourselves and into who God is. Smullyan in *The Tao is Silent* informs us that dogs have the Buddha nature. What does it mean to have the Buddha nature? The Buddha is at peace come famine or feast, and is compassionate towards self and others. In the same book, there is a haiku poem and commentary by Blyth:

> The puppy that knows not
> That autumn has come,
> is a Buddha.

The puppy even more than the mature dog takes each day, each moment as it comes. It does not

> Look before and after
> And pine for what is not.

When it is warm, it basks in the sun; when it rains, it whimpers to be let in. There is nothing between the sun and the puppy, the rain and the whimper.[7]

Watching my puppy, Dennis, teaches me a lot about who and what I am. I am reminded to laugh when something is funny; to cry when I am grieved; to play for the sole purpose of playing; to eat when I am hungry; to sleep when I am sleepy; and in this I am learning much about how to live a freer, more "abundant life."

5

Leadership

IT only takes a few minutes' reading to discover that the *Tao Te Ching* is a highly political book. The second half of the book is explicitly so, but it has political implications throughout. Presumably the document was used to instruct a young emperor in the art of good government. And instruct it does! If a government took the words of Lao Tzu as its constitution, it would result either in utter ruin or else in the greatest nation the world has ever known.

The *Tao Te Ching* says,

> The courts of law are far from the people's hearts. . . .
> But look, here are officials in elegant apparel
> carrying sharp swords
> Eating and drinking until they are bloated,
> Possessed of such wealth that they could never use it all.

Does this sound familiar? The president lives regally, making more than four times the average wage, while not fifty paces outside the White House, the homeless are trying to scrape together enough for day-old bread and a bottle of cheap comfort. This is indeed a government far from the people's hearts. Lao Tzu condemns such discrepancies when he says, "I call this positively criminal. / It is not the way of the Tao." Of what type of government would Lao Tzu approve? He would approve of one that is unobtrusive, moderate, and disdainful of war.

Unobtrusive Government

Like the founders of the United States' government, Lao Tzu believed that the government that governs least, governs best. Lao Tzu says: "Govern a big country as you would fry a small fish." Stephen Mitchell's version adds: "You spoil it with too much poking!" We could balk at Mitchell's liberties with the text, but the point his witty paraphrase makes is valuable. "When a government is unobtrusive / The people are simple and honest. / When a government is suspicious and strict / The people are discontented and sneaky." Lao Tzu has undying faith that people who are truly trusted will be truly worthy of such trust. If the government keeps its nose out of private people's affairs, the people will be happy and will have no reason to act inappropriately. Simple folk manage the simple affairs of their lives, and if government is anything to them it is something "away out there" that is really of little concern to them.

Such a government might have been possible in pre-industrial China, but we should question the efficacy of Lao Tzu's advice in the modern post-capitalist "first world." The present trend towards government de-regulation might be encouraging, but we can't ignore the shadow-side of such developments, which could give industry more license to poison the environment and exploit the poor.

The second part of this verse, however, needs no justification. We all sympathize a little with the average Joe who gets caught cheating on his taxes. After all, who understands the poor more than the poor, and many of us would give cheating ample consideration if we thought we could do it with impunity. Our government *is* suspicious and strict. No pay period passes without a percentage reminder, and that serves to promote general discontent (and more average Joes dodging for tax relief). Taken to logical extreme, this type of government becomes the nightmare of Orwell's *1984*. Big Brother is always watching, and the common people must resort to legal indiscretions to connect with some scrap of humanity. Orwell's nightmare is a powerful myth for us, for we have come too close to the truth of this story to shake it off as mere fantasy.

Imposition of a Single Will or Power Over

The problem of obtrusive government boils down to this: "Loving all people and leading them well, / can you do this without imposing your will?" It is the imposition of the will of one, the ruler/president/emperor that is the culprit here. There are also two criteria, loving people and leading them well. These are the ends toward which government is the means. Leading well should flow like deep water; it should not be a struggle, especially such a struggle as would ensue in the case of one person imposing his or her will on others, implying force and pain and, at best, resentment.

> The best leader is one that the people are barely aware of.
> The next best is one who is loved and praised by the people.
> Next comes one who is feared.
> Worst is one who is despised.

It is interesting that Lao Tzu bases his evaluation of a leader on popularity. We might even balk at this. Some of our most notorious presidents, for example, have been held in very high esteem by the general public. But though there is indeed a great distance between the best and next best, the third best justifies the order. A leader who is feared is a tragedy waiting to be played out. It implies that the people are aware that they are being lied to, led along with selected bits of information, and in other words *being manipulated by a leader imposing his or her will.* One cannot love the people and lie to them. One cannot lead well behind a *status quo* facade.

This principle extends into religious leadership as well. Hierarchical church structures are notorious for imposing an alleged divine law on the people of faith and, especially in our own time, in an effort to maintain power. The fear of God's wrath has been held over people's heads for centuries, and cannot help but to create a love-hate relationship between the human and the institutionally-sanctioned image of the Divine. One could argue that any faith that is built upon fear is an invalid one. Certainly it is not an ideal one. Such an arrangement is ultimately destructive to the institution and the individual. It is one that says, "Only I, your leader, know what is right," therefore limiting wisdom to the capacity of one person's experience, and most foolishly rejecting the abundant wisdom of the multitudes. Alan Watts notes that,

> When it comes down to it, government is simply an aban-
> donment of responsibility on the assumption that there are
> people, other than ourselves, who really know how to manage
> things. But the government, run ostensibly for the good of
> the people, becomes a self-serving corporation.[1]

The multitudes are assumed to be gullible and ignorant, certainly not trustworthy with power. Yet, Lao Tzu says, "If the leader does not have enough faith in the people, / They will not have faith in him [or her]." Faith, or trust is an integral part of any relationship. Without it, in fact, there can be no relationship.

Working Together, or Power-With

"The best leader puts great value in words and says little / So that when his work is finished / The people all say, 'We did it ourselves!' " Words are worth very little today. Our leaders pour forth an enormous volume of information both written and spoken, and yet actually manage to say little. If much more time were spent doing rather than saying, perhaps greater progress might be made. But Lao Tzu suggests that the leader work quietly so that the only noise is made by the people. Power isn't wielded, but delegated, spread around. This is "power-with"—power that is shared with others. When the people do the work, they are satisfied, both with themselves and with their leaders. The leaders really just stayed out of their way long enough to let them do what needed to be done. And this is the secret: It is not that the leader should not move the group in a desired direction, but that the people must be wooed, allured, not forced. Forcing will incite conflict. Seduction incites delight. Therefore the leader makes the ends desirable and also lets the people do the work. He or she gets out of the way, and lets the people go about theirs.

Not Leading

"As a leader," Lao Tzu says, "lead properly. / Don't resort to force in the usual ways. / Win the world by 'not-doing.' " Here we run into a friend from another chapter, non-action. As you recall, inaction is the way of yielding to the way things are, not struggling or forcing. The way one directs, then, as we read earlier, is to "Deal with the difficult while it is still easy. / Begin great works while they are small." This demands great foresight, however, clarity of vision and genuine wisdom.

True understanding of the Tao is not dangerous. It cannot be used for evil purposes because evil inevitably defeats itself. Because it lacks love, evil lacks the virtues, the insight and the will to sacrifice of itself. It lacks the patience that love gives birth to and is, by its very definition, devoid of true wisdom. More than this, though, the leader who follows the Tao will have no hidden agenda, because he or she has no desires, and is guided by the Tao itself.

> Therefore the Sage who leads says:
> "I practice 'not-doing' and the people transform themselves.
> I enjoy peace and the people correct themselves.
> I stay out of their business affairs and the people prosper.
> I have no desires and the people, all by themselves,
> become simple and honest."

The key to successful government, then, is in having leadership that is rooted in the Tao. For,

> If governments and leaders can abide in it
> All beings shall gratefully behave likewise.
> We would have a Heaven on Earth
> And sweet rains would fall.
> The people would not need to be told,
> They would just naturally do what is right.

Moderation

Lao Tzu fortunately does not let us drift in impractical ambiguity; he has some actual, solid, three-dimensional advice: moderation.

Stated briefly and subtly, still it has far-reaching implications. He says, "In leading people and serving Heaven," (note that you cannot successfully do one without the other) "There is nothing better than moderation." This is a handy rule of thumb in any area of life. Certain pleasures are God-given and wonderful in moderation, but become unhealthy burdens if allowed to dominate our lives. The same is true of things that are normally thought of only as virtues, for in the book of Ecclesiastes Solomon wisely warned that we "be not righteous over much; neither make thy self over wise," lest we defeat the very purpose of religion and learning.

"When you organize, you must of necessity / use names and order. / But given that, you must also know where to leave off / naming and structuring. / Knowing when to stop, you can avoid danger." This directly addresses one of the cardinal sins of organizational structures: bureaucracy. One reason ordinary people hate dealing with government, from income tax to food stamps, is the mountainous load of paperwork invariably entailed. Everybody hates it—even people in the government—but it is there nonetheless. It is too easily capable of getting in the way and smothering the very programs and people it was installed to protect and serve. The government should serve the people, not the other way around.

The wise use of moderation should likewise extend to all areas of local and national government, church government, and personal self-government as well. "In moderation, one is already following the Tao."

Disdainful of War

No issue is of greater importance to a country than war. War is the biggest game with the highest stakes played out with human chips. War should be seen as, at best, an unfortunate necessity. At worst, it is a display of enduring and tragic adolescence.

Lao Tzu is consistent. His advice on war is similar to his advice on leadership in general: "A leader who is advised to rely on the Tao / Does not enforce his will upon the world by military means. / For such things are likely to rebound." This passage hints at the concept of *karma,* found in Hindu and Buddhist religions. Karma is believed to be the law of divine justice in the universe. It is similar to the physics axiom: "Every action has an equal and opposite reaction" or the more colloquial, "What goes around comes around." With karma, one's spiritual progress (or regress) is not limited to one life, but is applied toward one's next. With noble actions, a holy life is likely to lead to a more peaceful and spiritually superior life to come, while a life of sin and cruelty can only lead one to a more miserable existence. All evil rebounds upon the perpetrator. The Hindu can rest easy if a criminal is not immediately brought to justice. He or she can have faith in that in due time the evil deed will be punished and virtue rewarded.

For the Taoist, forcing things is the very definition of sin. And sin is bound to backfire. War itself is a forcing issue which cannot be avoided. The goal, therefore, is to enter warfare reluctantly, determined to do as little damage as possible. For "Wherever armies have camped / Thistles and briars grow. / In the wake of war / Bad years are sure to follow." The very fact that there has been a war, no matter how necessary, has ill effects. Even the land feels it and mourns.

Once again, Lao Tzu cautions us to moderation when he says, "a good leader accomplishes only what he has set out to do and is careful not to overestimate his ability." This implies that the leader is someone possessed of a genuine sense of mercy and humility. It is reminiscent of the Warmark's Code in Stephen R. Donaldson's *Thomas Covenant* books:

> Do not hurt where holding is enough;
> do not wound where hurting is enough;
> do not maim where wounding is enough;
> and kill not where maiming is enough;
> the greatest warrior is one who does not
> need to kill.[2]

"[A good leader] does what he must," says Lao Tzu, "He gets results, but not by force." This leads to the most innovative of strategies, and is covered in great detail in Sun Tzu's *The Art of War,* an entire book devoted to Taoist military strategy.

Why should force be avoided even in warfare? So that one may not grow strong. For "Things that grow strong, soon grow weak. / This is not the Way of the Tao." The way of the Tao is to remain young, in body and spirit. As we have seen, young things bend instead of breaking. Things that have become rigid and seemingly strong can be snapped like twigs. For example, armies that have conquered see themselves as strong. Once they think themselves invincible, they are more likely to be defeated. The future efficacy of the army is reliant on its own self-concept. Lao Tzu warns:

> Achieve your goal, but do not brag.
> Effect your purpose, but do not show off.
> Be resolute, but do not be arrogant. . . .
>
> What others have taught, I also teach:
> "The violent shall die with violence."
> This is my primary teaching.

We cannot help but notice the similarity to Jesus' rebuke of Peter: "all they that take the sword shall perish with the sword." (Matt. 26:52)

Finally, victory is not something to be proud of. Warfare, according to Lao Tzu, is a last resort. It is entered into reluctantly and withdrawn from as soon as possible, and with as little damage as possible. "Military officers should observe their duties gravely, / For when many people are killed / They should be mourned with great sorrow. / Celebrate your victory only with funeral rites."

The continuous flood of American films glorifying war heroes is truly disturbing. These Rambo-esque heroes play out violence with a comic-book casualness. But then, in the late eighties, Hollywood seemed to find a conscience. Beginning with *Platoon,* America was forced to take a long hard look at Vietnam. Finally, there was enough distance for some objectivity. The men who fought were no longer two-dimensional images, but humans with crushing moral dilemmas; boys who were pawns in a struggle in which they had no stake. War was finally being viewed as the violent barbarity that it is, possessing nothing of the romantic notions of glory portrayed in the past.

> [In war] there is no beauty in victory.
> To find beauty in it is to rejoice at killing people.
> Anyone who delights in slaughter will never find
> satisfaction in this world.

I see this trend in popular culture and I hesitate to find comfort in it, fearing it to be only a fashionable whim. If it is, it has not passed without doing some good in causing some to think, to feel. But I would like to think of it as another small step in the evolution of our species. This last century has seen such great strides: the abolition of slavery and the equality of women, the triumph of civil rights, a global consciousness of humankind as one people and the wildfire spread of democracy. It seems too much to hope for, and yet hope we must.

> Weapons are the tools of fear.
> They are not appropriate for a Sage
> And should only be one's last resort.
> Peace is always far superior.

6

Oneness

"MYSTIC" and "mysticism" are controversial words in most
Christian circles. This is partly because the latter word rarely
appears without the prefix "Eastern." "Eastern mysticism" is synony-
mous with popular conceptions of Hare Krishna cults and the occult;
and that is, I feel, a tragic mistake. Nearly all of these reactionary
opinions are a result of well-meaning caution and unfortunate ignorance.

In fact, mysticism means the search for, or enjoyment of, union
with God. This is hardly a dangerous concept, especially for members of one of the most inherently mystical religions in existence,
Christianity. Christians universally believe that the believer is
indwelt by the Holy Spirit, and that real and eternal union with God
is the very foundation of our faith. Unfortunately, this gloriously
Good News has been reduced to a simply cognitive recognition, and
the tremendously important *experience* of our union with God has
been tragically neglected. Protestants may be especially guilty of
this, but no knowledgeable Catholic can be ignorant of the long, rich
tradition of Catholic mystical experience. With notable exceptions
like Thomas Merton, mysticism in the Christian world seems to be
dying a quiet death. This is tragic, because the very essence of Chris-

tianity is its historical emphasis on lived experience. The New Testament isn't a doctrinal statement, but a living testimony of what the authors saw, felt, and experienced to the depths of their being. Paul wrote about situations that were real in the early Church, not abstractions. Christians believe that Jesus was not, as the Gnostics alleged, a disembodied spirit that only *appeared* to be man, but a living, breathing, sweating, hurting, *feeling* human being who entered into the whole of human life. If this were not so, perhaps we could ignore the experience of union with God. But there is yet a greater reason we cannot, for we hold that God himself united with this flesh.

After Jesus' resurrection and ascension, the Holy Spirit arrived with a dramatic entrance and gave the apostles yet another kind of divine ecstatic experience which was theirs for the whole of their earthly lives and should be part of the lived experience of ours. If it is not, then we are missing a valuable part of our heritage—so valuable, in fact, that the gradual exclusion of it from our Christian traditions has resulted in dangerous attitudes towards our neighbors, our own bodies, and to the Earth herself. This exclusion is in no small part responsible for the precarious position we find ourselves faced with at the twilight of the twentieth century.

We rob ourselves of great treasures when we ignore such important Christian writers such as Julian of Norwich, Hildegard of Bingen, Nicholas of Cusa, Meister Eckhart, Brother Lawrence, Saint Francis, Saint Ignatius, John of the Cross, Theresa of Avila, Evelyn Underhill, Charles Williams, and Thomas Merton. They are mystics, one and all, who have brought the breath of life to what has at times been a very repressed and oppressive tradition. What we must recognize is that mysticism is not a dangerous heresy, but an essential ingredient to vital Christian living.

This is not to say that there is no practice of mysticism at all in Christendom, it's just that no one has bothered to give it name and see it as part of the historical ministry of God's gracious union with his children. I am speaking of many prominent movements of our century, such as the civil rights struggles, the return to monasticism in Roman Catholic circles, and the Charismatic renewal in both

Protestant and Catholic bodies. The Holy Spirit is not easily repressed, and has a way of slipping through our artificial structures to surprise us.

The Protestant tradition has not been completely divorced from the Church's historical mystics, either. Martin Luther was greatly influenced by the Rhineland mystics, especially Meister Eckhart, and John Wesley fostered a deep respect for the mystical tradition in Christianity. The Anglican Church, too, has welcomed many elements of mysticism and has produced important writings on the subject in our own century. That the Protestant Church has forgotten, or worse, consciously rejected her mystical heritage has been called by one prominent Roman Catholic theologian "the great scandal of Protestantism." Matthew Fox has written, "Protestants do not know their own roots. They are out of touch with thirty-three percent of what inspired Martin Luther's prophetic criticism of the Western church."[1]

Reclaiming our heritage is an important step towards healing in the modern Church, in both Protestant and Catholic bodies. Once we have recognized the importance of mysticism in our own tradition, we are free to view the mysticism of other faith traditions as well. The desire within humans to enjoy union with the divine is universal. The various techniques and schools within the existing traditions are a result of our universal longing for our Beloved, and need to be understood as such. Every tradition has fostered a mysticism—and, indeed, how could it be otherwise? Even orthodox Moslems have not stamped out their own sect of mystics, the Sufis.

"One-ness" is the essence of mysticism, both Eastern and Western, and although this affords us a great deal of common ground with other faith traditions, Western mysticism is informed largely by Western theology and possesses a thoroughly Western flavor. The study of Taoism invites us to discover our own tradition of one-ness, and we err to avoid this discovery. For it is in this that the greatest mysteries of our heritage are made available to us, not only for our attempts at comprehension, but for our very ability to live truly Christian lives.

The *Tao Te Ching* says,

People of ancient times possessed oneness.
The sky attained oneness and so became clear.
Earth attained oneness and so found peace.
The Spirit attains oneness and so is replenished.
The Valleys attained oneness and so became full.
All things attain oneness and they flourish.
The ancient leaders attained oneness
And so became an example for all the world.
All of this is achieved by oneness.

The phrase "attained oneness" above has different meanings. "Attain" denotes not something which these things were once without, but a realization of how things are. Thus, when "the sky attained oneness," the sky realized its unity with all, and because of this, all was made clear to him. When the "Earth attained oneness" it realized its unity with all and this filled her with peace, and so on. It is interesting that the people, in earliest times, as described in the *Tao Te Ching,* didn't need to attain oneness: they already possessed it. How wonderful this must have been! Remember that to Lao Tzu, the ancients knew the Tao and how to live within it; it is the people of his own time (and ours) who have forgotten this truth and need to rediscover it.

Most Christians are surprised to learn that such ideas are not exclusive to Eastern philosophy. In fact, they are as old in the West as Christianity itself. Rooted in the deep mysticism of St. Paul, they go to the very heart of the greatest mystery of our faith, the incarnation.

"God is Everywhere"

When children ask, "Where is God?" most Christian adults are likely to answer, "Why, God is everywhere." The answer arrives in the mind of the child as a great and glorious mystery. To adults, however, this is a stock response which is forgotten as soon as it is uttered. We say it because it was, most likely, the answer we were given as children when we posed the same question. It holds none of the mystery for us now that it did for us as children. Why is this? Perhaps it is because we no longer believe it. It is an intellectual "fact," not a lived and perceived reality. It is proffered as an adequate answer for children, who cannot possibly conceive the complexity of the dualistic model our post-enlightenment mindset has bequeathed to us. I suggest that it is we adults who are not capable of conceiving a unitary model of reality handed down to us by our pre-enlightenment saints and theologians. We need to become "as little children" and carefully consider the answer we flippantly toss to the young.

If we faced the reality of God's presence in all things and in all places, the theological and doctrinal implications would seriously call into question many of our accepted positions.

> God is the most obvious thing in the world. He is absolutely self-evident—the simplest, clearest and closest reality of life and consciousness. We are only unaware of him because we are too complicated, for our vision is darkened by the complexity of our pride. We seek him beyond the horizon with our noses lifted high in the air and fail to see that he lies at our very feet.[2]

The Mystical Body of Christ

The above quote is from one of the greatest works on this subject, *Behold the Spirit: A Study in the Necessity of Mystical Religion*. In it, Alan Watts informs us that the "two essential principles of the Incarnation [are] the localization of the universal and the union of God with matter."[3] St. Paul is the first great mystical theologian. In Paul, we find a vision of the Church as the mystical body of Christ. "For we are members of his body, of his flesh, and of his bones." (Eph. 5:30) "For we being many are one bread, and one body: for we are all partakers of that one bread." (1 Cor. 12:12) Time and again Paul refers to Christians as those who are "in Christ Jesus," not, of course referring to the historical, physical Jesus of Nazareth, but the mystical body of Christ, made flesh in the community of believers.

This is basic New Testament theology, and though not normally thought of as being "mystical" as such, it is profoundly mystical. That the universal Church, past, present, and future, beyond denominationalism is one body through the common indwelling of the Holy Spirit is completely orthodox teaching. What is more unusual is the view that Christ is manifest in our individual selves. As St. Simeon Neotheologos wrote, "We become Christ's limbs or members, and Christ becomes our members. . . . Unworthy though I be, my hand and foot are Christ. I move my hand, and my hand is wholly Christ, for God's divinity is united inseparable to me. I move my foot, and lo! it glows like God himself." [4] This is a glorious vision and is, though not much spoken of, also wholly orthodox teaching. In us, the universal Spirit of God is localized in the here and now, because God is, by the indwelling of his Holy Spirit, in union with our physical being.

Christ In All Things

That the church is the localization of the eternal in the physical world does not, however, exhaust the implications of incarnational theology. St. Paul in his letter to the Colossians wrote, "[Christ] is before all things and in him all things hold together." (Col. 1:17 NIV) If I may speculate a bit, it seems to me that this is a biblical answer to a puzzling phenomenon in modern physics. Science knows that particles that make up the atoms of which we consist hold together, the electrons forming a field around the nucleus and so forth, but the great puzzle facing us is *why*. Why do the disparate particles cohere into atoms? Why don't they fly apart and dissemble all matter?

As J. B. Phillips writes,

> They have demonstrated before the whole world that what we call "matter" is in fact destructible. Those things that we formerly regarded as almost imperishable, such as armourplate and concrete, could, under certain conditions, be dissipated into vapour less substantial than the smoke from a cigarette. Indeed, since the whole stuff of our planet, animate and inanimate, is composed of variously arranged atoms, it is by no means unthinkable that some experiment or deliberate act might result in a chain-reaction, exploding, so to speak, every atom of which this world is composed.[5]

This is a horrifying potentiality, and more horrifying because we don't understand why they don't "explode" all by themselves, let alone by our initiation. So what is it that holds the universe together? What else but the very fingers of the Spirit of God, of Christ, in whom "all things hold together?" This is not an unbiblical concept, but it might prove problematical for some Evangelical schools who believe that only "the saved" are possessed of God. Further exploration of this will undoubtedly reveal different sorts of visitation and communion with God's spirit, such as charismatics who, although already indwelled by the Holy Spirit, also experience the Spirit coming upon them, as if from the outside.

This concept will no doubt become much more palatable, and indeed, it is already widely accepted among Catholic Christians (Roman, Orthodox, and Anglican), for whom union of the divine with the mundane is a central aspect of daily spirituality. For medieval Catholics the intellectual acceptance of this reality was secondary to the experience of it. Many medieval Christian writers are labeled "the medieval mystics" for this very reason. The experience of the presence of God in all things was for them an awesome intuitive mystery.

> God created all things in such a way that they are not
> outside himself, as ignorant people falsely imagine.
>> Rather,
>>> All creatures flow outward, but nonetheless remain
>>> within God.
>> God created all things this way:
>>> not that they might stand outside of God, nor
>>> alongside God, nor beyond God,
>> but that they might
>>> come into God
>>> and receive God
>>> and dwell in God.
>> For this reason everything that is, is bathed in God,
>>> is enveloped by God,
>>> who is round-about us all, enveloping us.[6]

This quote from Meister Eckhart is representative of the views of many of the medieval mystics. What is also very interesting about them is that, although their theology was profoundly incarnational, predisposing them toward a mystical experience of God, this knowledge of God-in-all is not a standard teaching but comes in the form of a revelation, a realization above and beyond official dogma.

Julian of Norwich is profoundly struck by the sudden knowledge of God in a mere hazelnut; that God is in the hazelnut, and by his love, sustains its existence. "The fullness of joy," wrote Julian, "is to behold God in everything."[7] Mechtild of Magdeburg says, "The day of my spiritual awakening was the day I saw and knew I saw all things in God and God in all things."[8] From early in the theology of the Eastern Church, this view of God as united with the cosmos came to be seen as a continuing incarnation of Christ. It is traditional to view the Biblical events of God becoming manifest materially as always being the Word, the Christ. When God appears in physical forms in the Old Testament (called "theophanies"), such as the angel wrestling Jacob or the fourth man in the fire with Shadrach, Meshach, and Abednego, Evangelical theology often defines these events as visitations of the pre-incarnate Christ. Likewise in Pauline theology, the Holy Spirit-filled Church is the body of Christ. Therefore, if all physical manifestations of the Spirit of God are associated with Christ, then the Spirit-filled universe is itself the Cosmic Christ.

In our own century, Catholic scientist and theologian Teilhard de Chardin wrote, "The presence of the Incarnate Word penetrates like a universal element. It shines at the heart of all things."[9] Therefore, according to Alan Watts,

> To man and to atom, to star-cloud and to earth, to sun and to snow crystal, to mountain and to worm, to sage and to fool, to saint and to sinner, God, to whom size and number offer no obstacle, gives eternal and inescapable union with his very Self. For in God to exist, to create, to love and to redeem are all one pure and simple act; they are himself. And the gift of union with God's own Self is the Logos, the eternal Word, incarnate in history and incarnate in the souls and bodies of men as Christ.[10]

The medieval mystics accepted this not because of theological proofs, but from direct experience. It did not, as some may complain, make God less special, but it infused all of the ordinary and mundane with the sacred. All of life became truly religious. All of life was lived "in God." Suddenly Jesus' words about ministering to the "least of these" as ministering to him are transformed from figurative language into present, literal reality. Christ's sharing of human burdens and sin and pain did not end with the ascension of Jesus of Nazareth, but is a continuing communion in birth and death and pain and joy and sin and redemption with all of Creation throughout all of time.

> God says:
>> Now is the time
>> to tell you where I am
>> and where I will be.
>
>> I am
>
>>> in Myself
>>> in all places
>>> in all things
>>> as I ever have been
>> without beginning.[11]

When God is perceived as present in nature, we begin to view nature very differently: with respect, with reverence. The implications of this new view of nature will be covered more fully later, but for now let us understand that when in our thinking God becomes one with nature, there is a shifting of attitudes about ourselves that allows us to begin to perceive ourselves as one with nature, too.

Although not having this theology to support it, most Christians (and other people, too) have a numinous experience when alone in the wild. Somehow, God seems closer there. We cannot go through the forest without a profound sense of God's presence and power. It is for this reason, even if unconscious, that most Church camps and retreats are held in wilderness settings. This is no mistake. For as Julian says, "Nature and Grace are in harmony with each other. For Grace is God as Nature is God. God is two in manner of working and one in love. Neither Nature nor Grace works without the other. They may never be separated." [12]

Pantheism?

Lest some readers fear that I am advocating an acceptance of pantheism (God is everything; everything is God), let me put such fears to rest immediately. What we are discussing, is in fact the very antithesis of pantheism. This would be a grave concern indeed if pantheism were the sole experience of the Christian mystic. It is not. Alan Watts explains:

> Sometimes the mystic feels that this Spirit . . . is insepa-rable from the immediate contents of daily experience, and on the basis of this intuition is often erected the theology of pantheism or immanentism. At other times he experiences Reality as something immeasurably other than himself and all created things, as a Being infinitely great, holy and splen-did, before whom the world as we know it appears ugly, gross, and evil. From this intuition comes the theology of transcen-dence. . . . Again there are times when Reality presents itself to him as something so alive and intelligent that he feels himself to be in communion with a person. At other times he is so impressed with its infinitude and mystery that anything so suggestive of man as personality seems an unthinkable limitation.[13]

For the Christian mystic, pantheism, though closely resembling the experience of God in the physical world, is ultimately inadequate for it does not allow the equally valid experience of God as transcen-dent; nor does the impersonal nature of the pantheistic God allow for the personal aspect of God revealed to us in Jesus of Nazareth. As suggested earlier, God is not one or the other, but both. The truth lies in the tension between the two, in the paradox itself.

Let us explore further the distinction between pantheism and the God of the Christian mystical experience. First of all, what do we call the Christian unitary intuition? Clearly, pantheism is inappro-priate. I suggest a term coined by K.C.F. Krause (1781–1832) for his own theological studies: pan-*en*-theism. The insertion of the Greek preposition "*en*" denotes that, unlike pantheism, where God is all, in pan*en*theism God is *in* all. Whereas in classic pantheism, to subtract God from the universe would leave nothing, with Panentheism subtracting the universe from God would still leave God in all his transcendence.

The subtraction of the universe, in panentheism, does not detract in the least from God. God is still, and wholly, God. As Geddes MacGregor defines it, "though God includes and permeates all of Nature, so that all Nature exists in God, nevertheless God's Being is more than, and is not exhausted by Nature."[14]

Panentheism furthermore is indicative of the personal nature of the Christian God. For pantheism, God's union with the universe is necessary. Since there is nothing that exists that is not God, anything that is, must of necessity be a part of God. But for the panentheist, since God is also transcendent and not equally reliant upon the universe for existence, God's union with the universe is a free gift, given not of necessity, but out of love for the Creation.

Incarnation

As one begins to process the concept of panentheism, it becomes clear that God is profoundly inclusive—how could anything possibly be "beyond" God? If there were something outside of God, we would be faced with a God possessing limitations; a God who is not infinite and all-pervasive.

Try though we might, we creatures cannot "other" ourselves from God. We are inescapably filled with God by virtue of his love for us and for all. God, "whether we like it or not, want it or not, know it or not" is united to us and is enfleshed in us.[15] Nicholas of Cusa wrote, "Divinity is the enfolding and unfolding of everything that is. Divinity is in all things in such a way that all things are in divinity."[16] For this reason we can begin to understand evil's repulsion of the divine; to be unable to escape divinity is, for evil, truly horrifying. For this reason, evil is in constant denial, and in denying God's love and presence and power, is trapped in a web of lies both to others and to itself.

The gift of union with all of Creation offers us an incredible opportunity to grasp something of the mystery of the incarnation and crucifixion of Christ. God loves symbols. It is his best means of making the invisible and the ungraspable both understandable and real to humankind. Therefore, as truths have from the dawn of time been embodied in story, God enfleshed the truth of his union with us in a story in first-century Palestine. In the words of Alan Watts,

> The eternal Word, the Logos, becomes flesh, making our nature his nature; he assumes our limitations, suffers our pains and dies our death. More that this, he bears the burden of our sins: that is *he remains in union with us even though we crucify him and spit on him; he continues to dwell within us and to offer, or sacrifice, our lives to God even though we commit every imaginable form of depravity.* In short, God has wedded himself to humanity, has united his divine essence with our inmost being 'for better for worse, for richer for poorer, in sickness and in health' for all eternity.[17] [Italics by author]

7

World and Self

A T this time what is important is that the people of the world are made conscious of our dire environmental crisis. We must somehow translate environmental fashion into real consciousness. For the truth is that all of life, on land, in sea and air depends upon our oceans for life. And yet we use it to dispose of our sewage, "out of sight, out of mind." We forget that polluting a small fraction of the oceans is all that is necessary to kill all marine life. In the early 1970s, German rivers bore nine billion cubic meters of pollution annually. France was responsible for eighteen billion cubic meters. Today, each and every day, 50,000 tons of waste are discharged into the Rhine.[1] And where do the deadly rivers flow? The ocean.

Our industries are sending noxious poisons into the atmosphere that fall to the earth as acid rain. The freshwater lakes of Canada and Scandinavia are being poisoned by the thousands, becoming so acidic that no life support is possible. In Sweden alone 18,000 of her 96,000 lakes are affected.[2] Canada and Scandinavia are being poisoned by American and Soviet industry. Add to this the grave danger to our groundwater and natural springs from the irresponsible disposal of nuclear and toxic wastes and it is not difficult to grasp our peril.

Our land fares no better. John Robbins points out that the historic cause of the demise of most of the world's "great" civilizations is the erosion of their topsoil. This is terrifying when we discover that in only three hundred years America has lost *75 percent* of her total topsoil, and each year continues to lose four million acres, the size of the state of Connecticut.[3]

We are also responsible for the extinction of countless life forms, found nowhere in the universe but here. When they are gone, they are gone forever. The extinction rate is expected to escalate. Since 1990, species have been getting obliterated at the rate of 10,000 per year.[4] By 2010, one quarter of all species on the planet may be extinct.[5] In the words of Chief Seattle, this would mean "the end of living and the beginning of survival."

In Stephen Mitchell's version of the *Tao Te Ching*, we read,

> When man interferes with the Tao,
> the sky becomes filthy,
> the earth becomes depleted,
> the equilibrium crumbles,
> creatures become extinct.[6]

The Earth is dying. It is in the throes of a completely preventable disease: pollution. The people of the so-called first world have been in denial a long time. The fallacy of "what you don't know won't hurt you" is tragically revealed in the deaths of those who live in the shadow of nuclear power plants and those who unknowingly drink from poisoned ground water sources. The poison we put "out of sight, out of mind" will undoubtedly return to haunt us. As Lao Tzu says, "The violent shall die with violence."

In chapter seven of the *Tao Te Ching*, we are told, "Heaven is eternal, and Earth is long-lasting. / Why are they so enduring? / Because they do not live for themselves." For too long the goal of those in the West has been to get as much as one can and do everything possible to keep it, regardless of the consequences to others. Like a dog growling when someone gets too close to its food, the United States continues to spend billions on defense each year. Why? If we have the fire-power to blow up the world once, why should we need to stockpile enough to destroy it 21,000 times over?

For the cost of two fighter aircraft ($45 million) we could install 300,000 hand pumps in Third World villages to give access to safe drinking water. For the cost of one Trident submarine ($1.4 billion) we could inaugurate a five-year program for universal child immunization against six deadly diseases, preventing one million deaths a year. For the cost of one nuclear weapons test ($12 million) we could train 40,000 community health workers in the Third world.[7] Sixty million people will starve to death this year, yet all of them could be fed with the resources that would be saved if Americans would only reduce their intake of meat by 10 percent![8]

Why do we allow this to happen? Listen to Lao Tzu:

> Nowadays people don't bother with compassion
> But just try to be brave.
> They scoff at moderation
> And find that they have little enough for themselves.
> They step on people in their rush to be first—
> This is death!

He can hardly be more emphatic. "This is death." In short, according to Wes Granberf-Michaelson, "the world as a whole is not working. It is not working for the millions of people afflicted with economic deprivation. . . . It is not working for the forests, animals, water, and land that are in fights for survival."[9]

As a culture we have created a lifestyle myth that is pure fantasy. All our efforts are directed in living out this cultural lie regardless of its consequences. As Christians, we have participated in an even greater psychology of denial. Millions of dollars and work hours pour into missions the world over for the sake of "converting the heathen" to our own peculiar religious formula. We forget the Sermon on the Mount where the Son of Man at the judgment divides the sheep and the goats. To the goats he did not say, "Depart from me, ye cursed, for you did not teach me 'the sinner's prayer' or explain the 'Four Spiritual Laws.'" As scripture reports, he said,

> "I was hungry and you gave me nothing to eat, I was thirsty and you gave me nothing to drink, I was a stranger and you

did not invite me in, I needed clothes and you did not clothe me, I was sick and in prison and you did not look after me."

(Matt. 25:41-43 NIV)

How can we fail to recognize this? How can we so have perverted the Gospel? How long can we lie to ourselves, our neighbors and our God? This tragedy was felt by Hildegard of Bingen as far back as the twelfth century:

> Now in the people
> that were meant to green,
> there is no more life of any kind.
> There is only shriveled barrenness.
>
> The winds are burdened
> by the utterly awful stink of evil,
> selfish goings-on.
>
> Thunderstorms menace.
>
> The air belches out
> the filthy uncleanliness of the peoples.
>
> There pours forth an unnatural,
> a loathsome darkness,
> that withers the green,
> and wizens the fruit
> that was to serve as food for the people.
>
> Sometimes this layer of air is full,
> full of a fog that is the source
> of many destructive and barren creatures,
> that destroy and damage the earth,
> Rendering it incapable of sustaining humanity.[10]

The Theology of Domination

Hard as it is to hear, our theology is largely responsible for our society's attitudes. Chief Seattle summed it up when he said,

> We know that the white man does not understand our

ways. One portion of land is the same to him as the next, for he is a stranger who comes in the night and takes from the land whatever he needs. The Earth is not his brother, but his enemy, when he has conquered it, he moves on. He leaves his fathers' graves behind, and he does not care. He kidnaps the earth from his children, and he does not care. His fathers' graves, and his children's birthright, are forgotten. He treats his mother, the earth, and his brother, the sky, as things to be bought, plundered, sold like sheep or bright beads. His appetite will devour the earth and leave behind only a desert.

The theology we have inherited is called "the theology of domination." This is initially taken from the Genesis account where Adam and Eve are charged to "replenish the earth and subdue it: and have dominion over the fish of the sea, and over the fowl of the air, and over every living thing that moveth upon the earth." (Gen. 1:28) Therefore it is our charged duty to subdue the planet; it is a curse to Adam who must eat only by the sweat of his brow, instead of the blessing which God had intended. But by assuming ourselves to be God, having absolute rule over all of Creation, it is *we* who have cursed the earth, not God. Sean McDonagh in his book *To Care for the Earth* makes a strong point in that in the Middle Eastern Biblical culture, this kind of language makes a lot more sense than it does in Europe or North America. "In order to survive in the sparse mountains, barren deserts, steppes and narrow plains, human beings had to channel all their efforts into dominating, controlling and taming the natural world."[11] It is natural, then, for Middle Eastern cultures to make a marked distinction between Deity and Creation. This is especially notable in religions which have remained geographically restricted, such as Islam, but it has softened to a small degree among Jews, scattered into Europe by the Diaspora and Christians. It is softened, but is still the drive behind our ideology.

For many Christians this kind of theology gives us license to exploit God's Creation in any fashion that will benefit us. For fundamentalists, whose eschatological orientation is solely future-directed, it should be of little concern to us or to God what happens to the earth, since the end of the world is imminent. Setting all their sights on a future-based redemption, they neglect the redemption of the past and the present which Jesus purchased on the Cross (Col. 1:20). Since they believe "the Lord may return tomorrow," it does not matter what we do to the Earth today. Such theology is often a smokescreen to avoid ecological responsibility. Nearly every year there is a preacher somewhere who claims to know when the return of Christ will be, regardless of Jesus' words in the Revelation, ". . . thou shalt not know what hour I will come upon thee." (Rev. 3:3 KJV)

What if the Lord delays yet another thousand years? What about our planet then? What about our children? Our grandchildren? American Indian culture measures the morality of an action by how it affects the children seven generations hence. If we used such a standard, would we have pillaged three-quarters of the earth's riches in one generation? McDonagh warns us that, "as Christians we must be very watchful lest the mythic aura which surrounds any of our religious ideas about the world contributes in any way to the destruction of the Earth."[12]

We must create or rediscover deep within our tradition a theology of cooperation with nature rather than domination over it. No ecological movement will succeed until our worldview changes, and worldview is largely religious in nature. In fact, the United Nations Environment Program and the World Wildlife Fund have both made appeals to the world's major religions to help in addressing the environmental crisis from a spiritual perspective.[13] As Thomas Berry says,

> Presently the Church has a unique opportunity to place its vast authority, its energies, educational resources, its spiritual disciplines in a creative context, one that can assist in renewing the Earth. . . . If this is not done immediately, then by the end of the century an overwhelming amount of damage will have been done, an immense number of species will be irrevocably lost for all future generations. Only by assuming this religious responsibility for the fate of the Earth can

the Church regain any authentic status either in the human or in the Earth process.[14]

Stewardship Theology

The largest theological movement with an ecological conscience is Stewardship Theology. It is based on the Yawhist creation account from Genesis 2 rather than the Levitical account of domination. This says, "The Lord God took the man and put him in the Garden of Eden to work it and keep it." (NIV) The Hebrew word for "keep" used here is *shamar,* meaning to guard, protect, and preserve. The Earth is seen as being given to us not to exploit and use as we like, but as a great treasure entrusted to us for safekeeping. Stewardship Theology demands that we repent from our prodigal squandering and return to a responsible and right relationship with the Creator and his creation. Says Granberg-Michaelson,

> A Christian commitment to God's creation, then, must challenge the dominant modern framework of thinking about the world and offer a new vision for societies, rooted in God's ongoing activity as Creator, Redeemer and Sustainer.[15]

The shortcoming of Stewardship Theology is that it leaves intact Christian theology's arrogance toward creation. We are still lords over it. Nicholas of Cusa informs us, however, that "The knowledge of this world, where you believe you have surpassed all creatures is actually a joke in the sight of divinity."[16] It is painfully obvious that although humankind has greater intellectual capacity than the creatures, we may be surpassed in wisdom by most of them. Stewardship Theology also implies, as Matthew Fox calls it, an "absentee landlord" status for God. God is still somewhere "away out there," not here. So our motivation is chiefly the charge given to us in Genesis.

Mysticism

A better theology is one that is based on *emmanuel,* "God is with us," and creation is overflowing with God. Mechtild of Magdeburg asks, "How does God come to us? Like dew on the flowers, like the song of the birds! Yes, God gives himself with all creatures wholly to me."[17]

Native religions see the world as Mechtild above, as brimming with the divine. When one sees the world as the vessel of the Divine, one's attitude cannot help but change. Suddenly, the earth is seen not as a thing to be used and thrown away, but as the container and bearer and bride of God. Lao Tzu asks us,

Do you want to own the World and improve it?
I don't think you can.
You see, the World is sacred.
It can't be improved upon.
If you try you will ruin it.

Why is the perspective of native traditions so different from ours? Besides purely theological reasons, the fact is that we don't live on the earth any more. We live primarily on cement and pavement. Singer/poet Bruce Cockburn says, "[If] you stare at too much concrete you forget the earth's alive." [18] To the native, the earth is bubbling with life; it swells up out of the very ground before his eyes. It is literally magic.

One of the implications of Jesus becoming a thing of flesh is that, not only has God been joined forever with his creation, but that all of creation has been taken into God.

McDonagh writes,

To live we must daily break the body and shed the blood of creation. When we do this knowingly, lovingly, skillfully and reverently it is a sacrament. When we do it ignorantly, greedily, clumsily and destructively it is a desecration. In such a desecration we condemn ourselves to spiritual moral loneliness and others to want.[19]

This loneliness could in itself be our end. Charles Williams says that Hell is an isolation we choose out of exclusive concern for ourselves. If we are concerned only for ourselves we will eventually be left with only ourselves. Chief Seattle said,

What is man without the beasts? If all the beasts were gone, man would die from great loneliness of spirit, for whatever happens to the beast also happens to man. All things are connected. Whatever befalls the earth befalls the sons of earth. The white man, too, shall pass—perhaps sooner than other tribes. Continue to contaminate your bed, and you will suffocate in your own waste.

The World as Self

It is not enough for humankind to be respected by nature as its caretaker, we must respect the Earth, for it is she who feeds us. What is lacking is relationship. Humankind lacks a sense of real relationship with the Earth, as if we were aliens not sprung from this soil. The truth is we are this soil. If it is true that all of the cells in our bodies (with the exception of brain cells) are replaced every seven years, then, allowing a year for grain to cycle through the animals we eat, as little as eight years ago every single one of us was nothing but soil, soil waiting to nurture a thin green shoot that would someday become us.

Nikos Kazantazakis writes,

> It is not you who call. It is not your voice calling from within your ephemeral breast. It is not only the white, yellow, and black generations of man calling in your heart. The entire Earth, with her trees and her waters, with her animals, with her men and her gods, calls from within your breast. Earth rises up in your brains and sees her entire body for the first time . . . [20]

So if love for beauty is not enough, if the command of God is not enough, if compassion for others and our descendants is not enough, if God filling up everything is not enough, maybe selfishness is: We must save the earth because she is us. We must realize the truth of the Buddhist doctrine of dependent co-arising: We are not separate from this earth. "I" refers not to this individual body, or even this individual soul, but to the Earth—indeed the Universe—as a whole. What a revelation to realize that the Universe is me, too! We are not set apart from creation, we are an integral part of it. We are not masters over the land and beasts, but their kin. We are flesh of one flesh, soil of one soil, soul of one soul.

In the *Tao Te Ching* we read,

> What we must do is see the whole world as our "Self."
> Only then will we be worthy
> of being entrusted with the World.
> Only One who values the World as his own body
> can truly rely on the World in return.

Right Livelihood

In Buddhist teachings one of the believer's responsibilities is right livelihood, the idea that how one lives and what one does to earn a living is important to his or her spiritual progress. This is something we Christians can learn from Buddhists. I know too many Christians, who work for chemical plants or military aeronautics manufacturers, who see no discrepancy between their work and their faith.

To live in right relationship with the Earth demands that we do something. Earth Days come and go but the dangers remain. They are here to stay unless we make some very real and heroic sacrifices. Farmer and ecologist Wendell Berry said,

> I don't think we can take [environmentalism] seriously until people begin to talk seriously about lowering the standard of living. When people begin to see affluence, economic growth, unrestrained economic behavior, as the enemies of the environment, then we can take it seriously. But people are saying 'Give us everything we want and a clean environment' and that isn't a possibility.[21]

Perhaps this is the cross that twenty-first century Christians must learn to bear. There have been few causes so noble. Every facet of life must be faced prayerfully. What are we to eat? What are we to wear? How are we to travel? How are we to produce power? How are we to carry our groceries? How are we to entertain ourselves? How are we to worship? To quote Berry again, ". . . there isn't any place . . . where you aren't on the front line of the battle. There isn't any place that somebody hasn't picked out for some kind of exploitation." [22] The *Tao Te Ching* instructs us to live simply, to "live close to the Earth. . . . / Let people return to simplicity, / working with their own hands. / Then they will find joy in their food / Beauty in their simple clothes / Peace in their living / Fulfillment in their traditions."

Something that we have forgotten is the concept of the Sabbath for beings other than the human. The air needs a rest, the forest needs a rest, soil needs to rest. Otherwise how can they heal? During the French Revolution a ten-day work week was instated. They stopped that silliness only when the horses died.

What is demanded of us is not going to be easy. It will mean creating a new culture. It will mean sacrificing our own luxuries so that others (the Earth included) can have necessities. As Lao Tzu writes, "The path into light seems dark. / The way ahead seems to go backwards. / The path into peace seems rough. / The greatest good seems to us empty." But Hildegard of Bingen makes us a promise:

> As often as the elements,
> the elements of the world
> are violated
> by ill-treatment
> so God will cleanse them.
>
> God will cleanse them
> through the sufferings,
> through the hardships
> of mankind.[23]

Mechtild has another:

> God has given me
> the power
> to change my ways.[24]

8

Holiness

HOLINESS is a word we tend to surround with a great amount of baggage. It can call up visions of heavenly splendor, whispering saints of legend, sentimental stories of extreme sacrifice, and the specter of puritanical abstinence from anything even remotely pleasurable. Yet, when we honestly face ourselves, we often laugh a little at these (and many more) caricatures. How many people through the centuries have swallowed these mythologies whole? With all sincerity, they have tried to live out these superhuman roles only to find (as anyone with wisdom and compassion might have told them) that such a life is generally impossible and the attempt often leaves one broken, wounded, and bitter. Holiness in the Christian tradition is much maligned, a concept used more as a controlling agent by religious authorities than as an ideal of Christian living. What exactly is the role of holiness then, and what does it really mean?

Sin

Although a general definition of holiness might be "the absence of sin," my concept would augment this by adding "and the presence of joy." For joy implies awe and mystery not present in mundane "happiness." Having thus defined holiness, how might we define sin?

Traditionally, sin is seen as an action (or lack of an action) which is somehow contrary to the will (or law) of God. The Taoist would agree with this definition. The will of the Tao is to be one with the Tao, to live as nature lives, in harmony with the rest of nature, with the Tao and with him or herself.

Taoists also have a concept of a "fall." Long ago, in the Edenic period of the ancients, the Universe and humankind were in harmony. But then humans began to "tamper" with nature and now we, their descendants, are faced with the responsibility of discovering anew how to live healthy lives of compassion and reverence for the Tao and all it contains. If we continue to go contrary to the Tao, we will experience one frustrating obstacle after another until our deaths. In the Taoist mythos, the concept of original sin is never taken to the extreme known in the West; it isn't a universal or eternal corruption of human nature, and such corruption is certainly not a blight upon Creation as a whole. For the Taoist, there are no personal "eternal consequences" as such, just an annoying, unfulfilled existence. Chuang Tzu tells us of the period before the "fall":

> In the age when life on earth was full, no one paid any special attention to worthy men . . . they were honest and righteous without realizing that they were "doing their duty." They loved each other and did not know that this was "love of neighbor." They deceived no one yet they did not know that they were "men to be trusted." They were reliable and did not know that this was "good faith." They lived freely together giving and taking, and did not know that they were generous. For this reason their deeds have not been narrated. They made no history.[1]

Not to be this way is what sets the Universe off balance, and this, to the Taoist, is sin. It is not unlike Jesus' two "great" commandments regarding our love for God, and for our neighbors as ourselves. (Mark 21:30-31) And since, as we have seen, the Earth and all that is in her is not only our neighbor but a part of us, Christians can agree with the Taoist that for us not to behave in a reverential way is also sin.

Characteristics of Holiness

If living in accord with the Tao is the absence of sin, the presence of joy is a life that flows smoothly without undue stress or striving. Lao Tzu tells us that one who lives such a life is

Not self-centered, [he or she] is enlightened.

Not self-righteous, [he or she] is a shining example.

Not self-glorifying, she accomplishes glorious things.

Not boastful, she grows large inside.

It is much easier for Lao Tzu (and for us) to relate to what the Sage is not. In describing what the Sage *is* Lao Tzu cannot say enough and is anything but succinct. Remember that it was much easier for the Jews to hear the Ten Commandments—restrictions on their actions—than for them to adhere to all the things the Torah tells them they should do. Let's examine both the *do's* and the *don'ts* of Taoist holiness.

Not Self-centered

As we mentioned earlier, in Asian cultures there are only subtle concepts of the individual; the family is the smallest division of society. The good of the family outweighs the good of the self. The good of the stranger is also important, regardless of whether respect or hospitality is reciprocated. Lao Tzu says, "the Sage makes good on his half of the deal / And demands nothing of others." The Sage is one who gives without thought of personal remuneration or even gratitude. It is all the same to him or her. Since the Sage is not attached to anything material, there is nothing he or she cannot part with, even, and perhaps most especially, to a stranger—or even an enemy. In Luke's gospel, Jesus says similarly, "But love your enemies, do good to them, and lend to them without expecting to get anything back."(Luke 6:35 NIV) The Sage is not concerned with getting anything back because with the Tao all things flow out and return. Jesus continues in verse thirty-six promising that "your reward will be great." Lao Tzu concurs and adds wryly, "Heaven doesn't choose sides. / It is always with the good people."

The Sage gives of self in non-material ways, too. He or she is a model of compassion. "The Sage's heart is not set in stone. / She is as sensitive to the people's feelings as to her own." We in the West have not developed the discipline of compassion as have our brethren of Eastern faiths. For them, compassion is the very highest value to which the believer can aspire. In Buddhism, compassion is what moved Buddha to sacrifice his own spiritual gain in order to help others find the way. Compassion seems to be a universal constant in the spiritual life of humankind. To identify with the suffering, which Jesus did throughout his ministry and in his death—and continues to do with the poor, the hungry, the homeless and the oppressed— is the very heart of the Gospel.

"To people who are good," the Sage says, "I am good. And to people who are not good? I am good to them, too." This is reminiscent of Jesus's words in Matthew 5:44, "Love your enemies, bless those who curse you, do good to those that hate you and pray for those who persecute you." Lao Tzu's version is a comment on what is true for the Sage; it is not a directive. Jesus, however, gives us a command which carries with it great responsibility and equally great difficulty. When we ask ourselves why this is so difficult, we find that it is because of that old dragon, desire. It is because we are concerned with the self, the person inhabiting this skin, and not concerned with the Self that embraces all of Creation, the World as Self. We need to provide for the Self which includes all humans, all species, maggot to marsupial, and the very Earth herself. It is identity solely with the smaller, individual self that is the culprit.

> From birth to death,
> Three people out of ten are celebrators of Life.
> Three people out of ten are the advocates of Death.
> The rest simply move numbly from cradle to grave.
> Why is this?
> Because they are overly protective of this life.

These words should ring true for most Christians. Jesus said, "For whoever wants to save his life will lose it, but whoever loses his life for me will find it." (Matt. 16:25 NIV) Losing one's life means surrendering it to God, for service, for ministry to the larger Self— all the little selves and all of Creation. In this there is real life. And this is not only spiritual service, either, but in ministry to the larger Self the hungry are fed, the sick are cared for, the oppressed are freed and Creation goes on with the cycle of death and new birth. "In losing," says Lao Tzu, "much is gained."

Not Self-Righteous

This is a matter of great sorrow within our tradition. The Pharisees against whom Jesus railed during his ministry are still with us, still praying publicly on street corners and on television. Spiritual pride is a grave sin, one that is seldom addressed from the pulpit or even in print. This is perhaps because it is too painful an issue, too close to home, too common to all of us. Most of us are unfortunately unconscious about it. We may feel that we would never lord our spiritual superiority over others, but how many times have I walked out to my car on Sunday mornings hoping the neighbors might see me holding my Bible or my prayer book? How many times have I hoped other shoppers would notice my "God Rules" button or other drivers, the ΙΞΘΟΣ fish on my car? We can feel good about these things on one level, hoping that others may notice and give us an opportunity to share our faith. More often, though, it creates a barrier of seeming piety beyond which most people are not willing to look.

C.S. Lewis, in his classic *Mere Christianity,* observes that the best Christian witness comes from one who doesn't seem particularly religious. This is a curious observation. If we push our faith to establish our integrity, in our pride, we sabotage our own intentions. Faith and integrity are not of necessity related and certainly not in the mind of the non-believer; in fact so poor is our witness historically that to make even a modest show of our faith will most likely be interpreted as hypocrisy. If we live as Christians ought to live, then our integrity will establish itself, and once we have the respect of our peers, they will see us as unique among their experience of other Christians.[2]

Lao Tzu describes the Sage as one who is "honest, but not judgmental. / Strong, but not injurious to others . . . / Therefore the Sage knows himself, / but he is not opinionated." What is addressed here chiefly is respect. Sadly, Christians are notorious for disrespect to others when it comes to issues of faith—from the horrors of the Inquisition to the witchcraft trials at Salem, from the out-of-hand dismissal of any sacred tradition other than our own, to our refusal to hear the stories of others that are filled with pain because of religious oppression. All too often, it turns out to be *our* religious oppression. What we historically accomplished by the sword is now accomplished by the tongue from the pulpit. And it is still wrong. We have somehow been duped into believing that conversion is always an instantaneous occurrence. In my own experience I find that this is almost never the case. Conversion is a slow, difficult process. The seeds that were planted years ago slowly take root, and even more slowly blossom. Most of the time we are not aware of just when conversion occurs. More often we realize one day that what we felt last year, or five years ago, is not what we feel now.

God continuously calls all of humankind to himself, the Spirit constantly whispers and really needs little help from us. More often than not, we get in God's way, and though it may be for what we feel are the right reasons, we wind up hurting instead of helping.

What we must do is acknowledge that, know it or not, all people are being courted by God. Everyone's story is valid; it is *their* story. It is also their journey, their process. We need to honor people's processes, to see that what they are going through at any given time is exactly what they are supposed to be going through; and most of all we must trust that God knows what he is doing.

We fail when we do not. We fail in our ministry if we do not hear people's stories and do not honor their processes. We forsake them. We tell them, in effect, that we are only here for them on *our* terms. We must realize that where they are is where they should be and we are not relieved of our responsibility to love unconditionally or to respect that person's spiritual evolution. "Therefore," says Lao Tzu, "the Sage is always there to help people / So that no one is forsaken."

The Taoist, in seeing the universe as the balance of polar opposites, fully accepts not only his or her own dark side, but society's dark side as well. "What is a good person but a bad person's teacher? / What is a bad person but raw material for a good person?" This is something we would not be surprised to hear Jesus saying to the Pharisees when they confronted him for reveling with the sinners. Of course Jesus was reveling with sinners! For he "causes the sun to rise on the righteous and the unrighteous" alike. (Matt. 5:45) Jesus did not condemn the prostitutes and tax collectors. He befriended them and met them where they were so that the long task of conversion could begin. He respected them and was compassionate toward them. Both the wisdom of the Teacher and the "raw material" must be honored or else, Lao Tzu says, "You are greatly confused, / regardless of your intelligence."

If we look at our own spiritual journey as Christians as in no way superior to the journeys of others, we are capable of true ministry. It is spiritual arrogance that poisons the soul. Instead, the Christian mystic Mechtild of Magdeburg says that we should live "welcoming to all."[3] This welcoming is the standard of righteousness, not pious observances. "If you do not try to prove yourself superior to others, / You will be beyond reproach."

Not only are we guilty of not respecting the journeys of others, but we have very little compassion for ourselves when we fail to live up to the letter of the Law. This is another very destructive element in our tradition. To see ourselves as not righteous is to assume the judgment of God. This we have no authority to do. Holding up an impossible standard and demanding that other people also live up to it, is to imply that the person doing the demanding must live up to this standard. This is not an enviable position to be in. So instead we "put a good face on it" and become liars to the very family of God that is supposed to be there for our nurturing and support. J.B. Phillips wrote,

> . . . the conscientious, sensitive person who is somewhat lacking in self-confidence and inclined to introspection, will find one-hundred-percent perfection truly terrifying. The more he thinks of it as God's demand the more guilty and

miserable he will become, and he cannot see any way out of his impasse.[4]

When non-Christians see this sort of ego-destruction wreaked by Christians upon their very own, it is little wonder that they want no part of Christianity. How can we blame them?

"It is often more perfect," says Thomas Merton, "to do what is simply normal and human than to try to act like an angel when God does not will it. . . . It is not practical, it is not honest, it is not Christian to fly from 'every desire' and 'every pleasure' that is not explicitly pious."[5] Julian of Norwich assures us when she says,

> My own sin will not hinder the working of God's goodness. As long as we are in this life and find ourselves foolishly dwelling on sinfulness, our God tenderly touches us and joyfully calls us saying: "Let all your love be, my child. Turn to me. I am everything you need. Enjoy me and your liberation."[6]

Perfectionism is not righteousness, it is self-righteousness. Righteousness is the welcoming of all without judgment, including the welcoming of our individual self.

Not Self-Glorifying

Hand in hand with self-righteousness is self-glorifying, which is the opposite of humility. The word humility comes from the Latin word "humus," meaning earth. Lao Tzu tells us that we are to live "close to the Earth." This is as true in our attitudes as it is in our literal, bodily existence. Hildegard of Bingen said, "Holy persons draw to themselves all that is earthly."[7] What is earthly is what is in its natural state, not perverted by human contrivance. We should be earthy, most especially. This means being honest, even if we really want to impress someone; even if it is painful. This means being honest with ourselves about our motivations. If I were to give to a charity, would I be doing it out of philanthropy or out of a need to be affirmed that I am good? Too often, I fear, for myself the latter is usually the case. If I already felt like a good person, I would only give honestly, and would want no recognition of it from others. Lao Tzu says that, "the Sage works anonymously. / She achieves great things / but does not wait around for praise. / She does not want her talents to attract attention to her."

The Sage is also honest with him or herself in that he or she is not embarrassed if they don't know about something. It is typical for us to assume that we have God, his purpose, and our cosmology all figured out. This was the prevalent attitude in the European Renaissance, too, and the religious authorities condemned many of the scientists of the day (Copernicus, Galileo, etc.)—and anyone else who had courage enough to differ—as heretics. If we could still burn those who differ with us at the stake, it is a tragic truth that some of us would indeed leap at the offer. Note, for instance, the spokespersons of the "religious right" who today advocate the death penalty for homosexuals and women who have had abortions. The truth is that we really know very little for sure. The *Tao Te Ching* says that "She who knows that she does not know is the best off. / He who pretends to know but doesn't is ill." Our intellectual *hubris* is a disease that threatens to destroy us.

Becoming acquainted with not knowing is for many people very intimidating. When the black-and-white universe that has all of the answers is wrested from our grasp, we are in an often terrifying position which demands that we think. This is true terror, for many religious people have been taught not to trust themselves or to make up their own minds. As J. Henry Burnett has said in an interview, "There is no Christian position on abortion. Being a Christian does not relieve you of your responsibility to think."[8] When we are ready to accept a more ambiguous worldview we find life to be, oddly, much richer, more honest, more earthy. We find that we have much more in common with non-Christians and may discover that many of them are downright godly, or as Lao Tzu would say, sagely.

"Only someone who realizes he is ill can become whole," says Lao Tzu, "The Sage is not ill because she recognizes / this illness as illness, / Therefore she is not ill." This might seem to be double-talk, but it isn't. Once the illness has been named, it can be treated. Once we realize that we don't have all the answers and that we're no less petty and misled than non-Christians, we can start moving toward wholeness, and toward what it really means to be earthy and Christian.

Jesus, born in a stable and taking the body of a human being, is our shining example of someone who is not self-glorifying. He endured the indignity of beating, nakedness and death without revealing his glory. When questioned by the authorities, he did not claim to be God, but did not deny it when asked. He did not live with riches, but as a transient rabbi who begged for his food. He did not own a house, nor, apparently, did he want to. It seems almost impossible not to think of Jesus when Lao Tzu tells us, "One who accepts [(or bears)] a people's shame is qualified to rule it. / One who embraces a condemned people / is called the king of the Universe."

Grounding and Embracing

"One who is well grounded will not be uprooted. / One who has a firm embrace will not let go." Grounding and embracing are essential qualities of holiness. One who is grounded in the earth will be earth-centered, not self-centered. He or she will do what is right and holy for others, for the planet, rather than what will benefit him or her directly.

One who embraces the whole of life will not slip into self-righteousness. Their motivations will come from the inside rather than from what others are likely to think of them. Eckhart says,

> Even if it were God himself compelling you to work from the outside, your works would be dead. If your works are to live, then God must move you from the inside, from the innermost regions of the soul—then they will really live. There is your life and there alone you live and your works live.[9]

One who is grounded in the earth has no need to be self-glorifying, since the universe is also him or her, and has enough glory to go around. Accomplishing great works is not enough, for they are empty victories. As Teilhard de Chardin tells us,

> Do not forget that the value and interest of life is not so much to do conspicuous things . . . as to do ordinary things with the perception of their enormous value.[10]

Holiness is the perception that all of life—even washing dishes as Brother Lawrence did—is holy. Labor and recreation are holy. All that we do should embrace life as it presents itself to us, the good and the bad. All that we do should be grounded in the earth, motivated by the good of the whole of Creation that is also us.

One who stands on tiptoe does not stand firm. . . .
One who considers himself righteous, isn't. . . .

One who is well grounded will not be uprooted. . . .

Cultivate these things in yourself
And you will have true goodness. . . .

Cultivate these in your community
And goodness will catch on. . . .

Cultivate these in the World
And goodness will fill the Universe.

And so, let the self examine the self. . . .
Let the community examine the community. . . .
Let the World contemplate the World.

How do I know the World is like this?
Through these:

Grounding and embracing.

EPILOGUE

W E are excitable beings, we humans. The greatest joy we can experience is when we take what is already a genuine joy and share it. I make no excuses for the *Tao Te Ching*. It has been a great inspiration to me and one of those genuine joys. It communicated things to me that I didn't know were already deep in my Christian heritage. It awakened that which was dormant and gave much light where it had been dim. I will always be grateful to my friend for lending me his cherished copy, and I hope that I have, in writing this book, returned the favor.

It was a book that had to be written. Few Christians of their own accord would probably even open a copy of the *Tao Te Ching*, feeling it to be false teaching or irrelevant to their own faith. Many would even be frightened of it. I hope that the experience of the reader has been a good one, and that this book will be passed along to others.

We are challenged in the next millennium with the very serious business of living together as a community with understanding, compassion, and encouragement. But there can be no encouragement without compassion, and there can be no compassion without understanding. Without understanding there is only fear, and of fear we have quite enough. The fundamentalism that is sweeping the

West is the result of this fear. The world is too complicated; people need to believe in something simple, something concrete. This is what the fundamentalist version of God provides: an easy set of *do's* and *don'ts* and little license to think. But this simplistic solution is no solution. It does nothing to reflect the complex and ambiguous nature of our world. We will not learn to live together by burying our doctrinal heads in the sand. We must meet the foe—ignorance, fear, and the unknown—bravely. Our faith traditions are our very foundations. We need them. We cannot by any means meet the foe without them. They are all that we are. We also need one another. Our faiths in isolation will not meet the challenge; each time we insist that our faith alone will save the world, ignorance and fear grow stronger. If our image of God serves to perpetuate tribalism, hostility, and bigotry, then our image of God must go. Scripture says, "by their fruits you shall know them." Of the fruits of religious absolutism we are painfully aware. Meister Eckhart says, "I pray God to rid me of God. The highest and loftiest thing that one can let go of is to let go of God for the sake of God."[1] If we are to enter the twenty-first century whole, our tribalistic image of the divine must break out of its box. The purpose of interfaith dialogue is to begin to approach the Ultimate Reality which transcends our cosmetic differences, to attempt to feebly grasp That which is beyond our ritual traditions and texts.

We cannot come to the table of interfaith communion with the opinion that we are in some way God's "special people." If so, then the brethren beside us are God's "other special people," and if true dialogue is to ensue they cannot be any less. By looking through their eyes we see much that our own tradition has blinded us to. If the *Tao Te Ching* is helpful to us, we need to read the *Talmud,* too. And the *Bhagavad Gita,* the *Upanishads,* and the *Dhammapada.* In this the world is truly our oyster.

> This mist, this cloud, this darkness
> into which we go, transcending knowledge,
> is the path below which your face cannot be found except veiled;
> but it is that very darkness
> which reveals your face is there, beyond all veils. . . .

The Lord of Sky and Earth has heard the groans of those
who have been slaughtered
and imprisoned and reduced to slavery
and who suffer because of religious wars.

And because all of these, who either are the persecutors
or the ones persecuted, are motivated by the belief,
that this alone is necessary for salvation
and pleasing to the Creator.

The Creator is moved with compassion towards humanity
and will try to guide all the variety of religions
to one greater unimpeachable harmony
in which all opinion is one.

—Nicholas of Cusa[3]

I am not advocating a unity of religions—far from it. If that were
to happen, each of our traditions would be irredeemably impoverished. What I am advocating is a unanimous celebration of diversity.
Diversity is a gift—just look at God's myriad and bizarre creatures!
Our traditions, too, are myriad, and we do seem to each other bizarre. It is because of this, that we have explored such divergent
paths of divinity and humanity, that we have so great a wealth to offer
to one another. And it is the God of my experience that teaches me
this. W.C. Smith says,

> The God whom Christ reveals is a God of mercy and love
> who reaches out after all men and women everywhere in
> compassion and yearning; who delights in a sinner's repen-
> tance, who delights to save. It contradicts, I admit, certain
> man-made formulations of Christian theologians, to say this;
> but it contradicts the central revelation of Christ to say any-
> thing else. If St. Paul or anybody else thought or thinks that
> only Christians can be saved, St. Paul was wrong. It is Christ,
> and the God who has given me faith through Christ, that save
> me from believing so blasphemous a doctrine. . . . If it had
> turned out that God does not care about other men and
> women, or was stumped and had thought up no way to save

them, then that would have proven our Christian understanding of God to be wrong.[3]

The force of Dr. Smith's statement is appropriate: enough is
enough. The God of the experience of most Christians is in varying
degrees different from the party line they hang on. My experience
agrees with Mechtild of Magdeburg: "God has enough of all good
things except one: of communion with humans God can never have
enough."[4]

Reading the *Tao Te Ching* is sort of a primer. And we all need an
education when it comes to building a common world, where diverse
ethnic and traditional elements are respected and celebrated. Such
wealth is out there to be discovered! Teilhard de Chardin tells us that
"Christianity does not ask us to live in the shadow of the Cross, but
in the fire of its creative action."[5] It is up to this generation to find
the courage to meet our fears and find our friends, for if we don't
there will be no future generations.

> The age of nations has passed.
> Now, unless we wish to perish
>> We must shake off our old prejudices
>> and build the Earth.

—Teilhard de Chardin[6]

NOTES

Introduction

1. Holmes Welch, *Taoism: The Parting of the Way* (Boston: Beacon Press, 1957), 1–2.

2. Thomas Merton, *Mystics and Zen Masters* (New York: Farrar, Strauss and Giroux, 1961), 73.

3. Quoted by Murray Stein in "Jung's Green Christ," in *Jung's Challenge to Contemporary Religion,* ed. Murray Stein and Robert L. Moore (Wilmette: Chiron Publications, 1987), 8.

4. W.C. Smith, *Towards a World Theology: Faith and the Comparative History of Religion* (Philadelphia: Westminster Press, 1981), 90.

5. John S. Dunne, *The Way of All the Earth: Experiments in Truth and Religion* (New York: Macmillan Publishing Co., 1972), 127.

6. Blanche Marie Gallagher, ed., *Meditations with Teilhard de Chardin* (Santa Fe: Bear and Company, 1988), 120.

7. Dunne, ix.

8. Naomi Stone-Burton, Bro. Patrick Hart, and James Laughlin, eds., *The Asian Journal of Thomas Merton* (New York: New Directions, 1975), 233–236.

Chapter 1

1. Carl Jung, "Answer to Job" (New York: Princeton/Bollingen, 1958), xii.

2. James I. Yockey, *Meditations with Nicolas of Cusa* (Santa Fe: Bear and Company, 1987), 68.

3. Smith, 153.

4. Ibid., 175.

5. See Is. 42:14; Is. 49:14-15; Is. 66:12-13; Hos. 11:1,4; Ps. 131:2,3. In the wisdom literature, Divine Wisdom is a woman (see Prov. 1:20-33; 8:1-36; 9:1-6. Also the Apocrypha: Wis. 7:27; 8:1).

6. Sue Woodruff, ed., *Meditations with Mechtild of Magdeburg* (Santa Fe: Bear and Company, 1982), 109.

7. Thomas Merton, *Conjectures of a Guilty Bystander* (New York: Doubleday Image, 1968), 294-295.

Chapter 2

1. Carrin Dunne, "Between Two Thieves," in *Jung's Challenge to Contemporary Religion,* ed. by Murray Stein and Robert L. Moore (Wilmette: Chiron Publications, 1987), 21.

2. William L. Dols, Jr., "The Church as Crucible for Transformation," in *Jung's Challenge to Contemporary Religion,* ed. by Murray Stein and Robert L. Moore (Wilmette: Chiron Publications, 1987), 140.

3. Yockey, 67.

4. Carrin Dunne, 16-17.

5. Bentley Layton, *The Gnostic Scriptures* (Garden City: Doubleday, 1987), 238.

6. Matthew Fox, O.P., *Meditations with Meister Eckhart* (Santa Fe: Bear and Co., 1983), 44.

7. Matthew Fox, O.P., *Original Blessing* (Santa Fe: Bear and Company, 1983), 49.

8. Ibid., 317.

Chapter 3

1. Camille Anne Campbell, ed., *Meditations with John of the Cross* (Santa Fe: Bear and Company, 1979), 15.

2. James Collins, ed., *Meditations with Dante Alighieri* (Santa Fe: Bear and Company, 1984), 19.

3. Fox, *Meditations with Meister Eckhart,* 61.

4. Ibid., 54.

5. Collins, 101.

Chapter 4

1. Thomas Merton, *The Hidden Ground of Love: Letters,* William H. Shannon, ed. (New York: Farrar, Strauss, Giroux, 1985), 627.

2. Benjamin Hoff, *The Tao of Pooh* (New York: Dutton, 1982), 68.

3. Welch, 33.

4. Woodruff, 118.

5. David Steindl-Rast "Recollections of Thomas Merton's Last Days in the West," *Monastic Studies,* 7 (1969), 2–3.

6. Quoted in Alan Watts, *Behold the Spirit: A Study in the Necessity of Mystical Religion* (New York, Random House, 1972).

7. R.H. Blyth, *Haiku* (Hokuseido Press, 1952).

Chapter 5

1. Alan Watts, *Tao: The Watercourse Way* (New York: Pantheon Books, 1975), 81.

2. Stephen R. Donaldson, *Lord Foul's Bane* (Garden City: Doubleday, 1977), 232.

Chapter 6

1. Matthew Fox, O.P., "The Great Scandal of Protestantism," *Creation,* (May/June 1985), 6.

_____

2. Watts, *Behold the Spirit,* 91.

3. Ibid., 80.

4. Quoted in ibid., 82.

5. J.B. Phillips, *Your God Is Too Small* (New York, Collier Books, 1961), 66.

6. Fox, *Meditations with Meister Eckhart,* 22.

7. Brendan Doyle, *Meditations with Julian of Norwich* (Santa Fe: Bear and Company, 1983), 60.

8. Woodruff, 42.

9. Gallagher, 107.

10. Watts, *Behold the Spirit,* 87.

11. Woodruff, 30.

12. Doyle, 108.

13. Watts, *Behold the Spirit,* 128.

14. Geddes MacGregor, *Philosophical Issues and Religious Thought* (Boston, Houghton Mifflin, 1963), 128.

15. Watts, *Behold the Spirit,* 74-75.

16. Yockey, 29.

17. Watts, *Behold the Spirit,* 74.

Chapter 7

1. Sean McDonagh, *To Care for the Earth* (Santa Fe: Bear and Company, 1986), 41–42.

2. Ibid., 23.

3. John Robbins, "Realities 1989": Facts excerpted from the Pulitzer Prize nominated *Diet for a New America* (Santa Cruz: Earthsave, 1989), 1.

4. McDonagh, 37.

5. Ibid., 35.

6. Stephen Mitchell, *The Tao Te Ching: A New English Version*

(New York: Harper and Row, 1988), 39.

7. Fox, *Original Blessing*, 14.

8. Robbins, 2.

9. Wesley Granberg-Michaelson, "Renewing the Whole Creation," *Sojourners*, (February/March 1990), 14.

10. Gabriel Uhlein, OSF, *Meditations with Hildegard of Bingen* (Santa Fe: Bear and Company, 1983), 77.

11. McDonagh, 111.

12. Ibid., 138.

13. Granberg-Michaelson, 11.

14. Thomas Berry, *Newsletter of the Center for Reflection on the Second Law*, no. 53.

15. Granberg-Michaelson, 14.

16. Yockey, 65.

17. Woodruff, 36.

18. Bruce Cockburn, "Standing Outside a Broken Telephone Booth with Money in My Hand," from the album *Further Adventures Of* (Toronto: True North Records, 1977).

19. McDonagh, 136.

20. Nikos Kazantzakis, *The Saviors of God: Spiritual Exercises* (New York: Simon and Schuster, 1960), 81.

21. Wendell Berry, interview in *The Progressive*, (May 1990), 34.

22. Ibid., 37.

23. Uhlein, 79.

24. Woodruff, 112.

Chapter 8

1. Thomas Merton, *The Way of Chuang Tzu* (New York: New Directions, 1965), 76.

2. C.S. Lewis, *Mere Christianity* (New York: Macmillan, 1954), 124.

3. Woodruff, 79.

4. Phillips, 31.

5. Merton, *Conjectures of a Guilty Bystander,* 21.

6. Doyle, 62.

7. Uhlein, 64.

8. T-Bone (John Henry) Burnette, "The Wittenburg Door Interview: T-Bone Burnette," *The Wittenburg Door,* (August-September, 1984), 22.

9. Fox, "The Great Scandal of Protestantism," 7.

10. Gallagher, 130.

Epilogue

1. Fox, *Meditations with Meister Eckhart,* 50.

2. Yockey, 107.

3. Smith, 170–171.

4. Woodruff, 56.

5. Gallagher, 78.

6. Ibid., 119.